A
Foundation of
Trust

Effective Models and Activities For Leaders,
Trainers, and Facilitators Engaging the Issues
of Trust and Trustworthiness

Sam Sikes

Copyright© 2014 by Sam Sikes
ISBN 978-0-9882046-5-2

DoingWorks, Inc.
351 CR 277
Liberty Hill, TX 78642
(512) 230-0969
Printed in the United States of America

Thank you

To all the training participants who willingly, or sometimes unknowingly, played "guinea pig" while I tested out new activities and model presentations...

To the trainers, facilitators, and leaders who helped and supported the writing effort despite my procrastination...

Specifically to BJ Penick, Ann Sikes, Chris Cavert, and Glen Olson; QuikTrip, Leadership Monroe, and Indiana Teen Institute for their valuable contributions...

Especially to my parents: My mom who taught me kindness and helpfulness, and my dad who taught me to leave things in better condition than I found them and "if you don't know it, learn it."

Table of Contents

Disclaimer

All activities contain some inherent risk of injury whether it be physical or emotional. The author has devoted reasonable attention to the safety of any activity included within this book by describing potential hazards and testing the activities with others.

The reader assumes all risk and liability for any loss or damage that may result from the use of the materials contained in this book. Liability for any claim, whether based upon errors or omissions in this book shall be limited to the purchase price of this book.

Introduction

In the beginning, I set out to write a book primarily for facilitators, trainers, and leaders to help them present the concept of trust in a relevant and influential way. The goal was to offer true views and understandable models that teach about trust and several activities people could experience to bring the viewpoints and models to life. I believe I have accomplished that goal, although it has been much more difficult than I imagined. Trust, while it is at the core of human interaction, has many parts. In the process of trying to define trust, I kept discovering new perspectives of trust that made it impossible to

> I decided to focus-in on trust as it relates to personal interaction with individuals and groups or teams.

fully describe in just a few organized sentences. Trust was even too big for a single book. With that in mind, I decided to focus-in on trust related to personal interaction with individuals and groups or teams.

Definitions of Trust

I often ask people in team building and leadership programs for a definition of trust. The responses are consistent. First, there is a long silence, as if I had asked them a trick question or maybe they had not ever really thought about it. Finally, the descriptions trickle out: Belief, honesty, faith, being there for someone...

The difficulty in defining trust in a plain and succinct way may be that trust has so many sides to it. It is a priceless jewel with many facets. We say trust in English, but other cultures and languages emphasize various aspects of trust. Below are a few of the many meanings that make up trust.

American Heritage Dictionary
Firm reliance on the integrity, ability, or character of a person or thing.

Anglo-Saxon
"trow" – trust or true, you can trust someone because they are true and truthful to you, also the origin of truce

Hebrew
chasah – lean on someone or something for support or take refuge in

batach and avatiyach – to cling to like a melon clings to its vine

yachal – to know something will happen in the future

aman – hold firm, hold a baby, sure, like putting a tent peg into firm soil so it's not pulled out by wind

mibtach – object of one's confidence, security

Greek
elpizó (pronounced "el-pid-zo") – to expect or confide in, hope for

peithó (pronounced "pie-tho") – to convince, persuade

pisteuo (pronounced "pist-yoo-oh") – to have faith in, believe

Swahili

> tumaini – hope (to want something to happen)
> muamana – confidence in or reliance on some
> person or quality

Chinese

> xìn (pronounced "shin") - trust with emphasis on
> being true to your words

For a good source of definitions, research, and lists on the topic of trust, look at the "World Database of Trust" compiled by Harvey S. James, Jr., Ph.D. at the University of Missouri (2007).

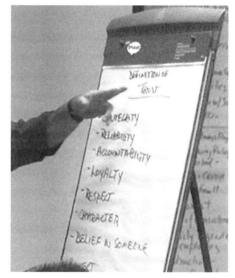

The following definition of trust I particularly like because it matches the focus of this book and includes both the attitude of the trust relationship as well as the behavior. It is also linked to the research done to form the Leadership Trust Model on page 34.

Trust is a psychological state in which one party is willing, "to be vulnerable to the actions of another party based on the expectation that the other will perform a particular action important to the trustor" (Mayer, Davis, & Schoorman, 1995, p. 712)

Models Of Trust

Because trust is full of important meaning, it is easy to become trapped in an academic discussion of its various meanings. It is important to focus on certain aspects of it and give it a functional purpose. I call it "giving it legs." The following models of trust do just that. They offer clarity to different aspects of trust and allow you to take action to develop trust in relationships. With the models, people can better understand the concepts of trust. And with the activities, they can try them out in a controlled environment. The following four models of trust are included in this book:

Trustworthiness

Another aspect of trust contained in this book is the topic of trustworthiness. As I researched other books and recalled my own experiences with trust, I came to the realization that trustworthiness is one facet of trust that each person can work to improve regardless of who is around them. Whether or not someone else trusts me, I can still do what it takes to be more worthy of trust. As far as personal development, becoming more trustworthy is certainly my responsibility and I can work to improve it anytime, no matter what my circumstances.

Trust Yourself?

Many people offer the advice to trust in yourself. A person may say something like, "At least I can trust myself." While this sounds like something that everyone

> A **fundamental attribution error** occurs when we overestimate how much another person's behavior can be explained by their temperament, attitude, or mood. It reflects failing to adequately consider the role of some situational factors that may affect a person's behavior.

should do, it is often communicated as if it's just a given. Truthfully, if we were able to objectively see ourselves, we might not trust ourselves nearly so much. How many times have you gone on a diet to lose weight, started an exercise plan, vowed to watch less TV, save more money, get more sleep, etc., then dropped it for any number of reasons? If you were looking at someone like that from the outside, you might not really trust him or her to follow through on commitments. Of course, since it is actually you, you can justify the behavior. This phenomenon is called a fundamental attribution error. That is the natural tendency for human beings to falsely attribute the negative behavior of others to their character, while attributing our own negative behavior to our environment. The one reason you can forgive so many of these broken promises you make is that you know your intentions. The willingness is there to do all of those things. Unfortunately, we don't often trust or forgive others because we only see their behavior. When they fail, we don't know their intentions for sure and so we guess. It is like the hardworking employee who was angry at his boss for overlooking him for a promotion. The employee saw his boss as mean-spirited and "trying to make him quit." However, the employee had not asked for a promotion, and furthermore, had no idea if there was even an available position or funds to make a promotion possible. The employee made the error of assigning all these "intentions" to the boss, yet had not even made the boss aware of his desires.

I am certainly not saying that we shouldn't trust ourselves, but it is simply not true that we can always trust ourselves. Strengthening our own character will help, and fortunately, we don't have to be perfect before we can develop trust with others. None of us is perfect, so forgive and apologize whenever the need arises so that you can move forward.

Why is trust so hard?
One reason it is hard to trust other people is that a few truly untrustworthy people exist in this world. Doubt and risk definitely interfere with trust. When was the last time you were asked to help a stranger from Nigeria transfer funds from a corrupt government? The following email was sent to me with the name of a friend typed at the top and bottom. Notice what the author does to gain my trust. The grammar and spelling have been kept the same as the original.

Sad News.......... (friend's name)

Hello,

This message may come to you as a surprise but I need your help.Few days back we made and unannounced vacation trip to Manila Philippines. Everything was going fine until last night when we were mugged on our way back to the hotel.They Stole all our cash,credit cards and cellphone but thank God we still have our lives and passport.Another shocking is that the hotel manager has been unhelpful to us for reasons i do not know. I'm writing you from a local library cybercafe. I've reported to the police and after writing down some statements that's the last I had from them.i contacted the consulate and all i keep hearing is they will get back to me. i need your help ..I need you to help me out with a loan to settle my bills here so we can get back home, our return flight leaves soon. I'll refund the money as soon as i get back. All i need is $1,950 ..Let me know if you can get me the money then I tell you how to get it to me.

I'm freaked out at the moment

Regards.

(friend's name)

It sounds like my friend is in a bad spot. She has lost all forms of communication (except this email), lost all the ways of making payments, and everywhere she turns she is getting no help. She has been very responsible talking to the police, the consulate, and the hotel manager. All she needs is money to do the upright thing and pay her bills. Of course, this is all a scam to get my money. My friend is actually at home with no plans of even going to Manila. But notice all the components that have been included in this email to get me to trust that it is true and I should respond. Her name is right in the email and she is really a friend I met in my travels. She's desperate. No one even knows she's out of the country and now, because her money was stolen, she needs help soon before her plane returns. What kind of friend would I be if I didn't at least say I could send some money? There is something desperate about her typing and she confirms that she is "freaked out."

Although this message is false, it does illustrate how someone can influence another person's ability to trust them when she shows she is in need of help and willing to be trusted. It must work at least some of the time or these phishing messages would not continue to be distributed. So should we stop trusting emails?...of course not. However, we have to use some common sense. I would hope that if a friend were actually in need of assistance, she would write to me more specifically. If she had mentioned when we had met last and asked about something one or both of us were working on, I might have been convinced.

How much trust is enough?

Suppose that you are trying to cross from one cliff to another one that is a hundred feet away. It is five thousand feet down to the rocks below. Fortunately, you have a one-inch thick piece of rope that is capable of holding up several tons. There is a difficulty though, because you have only fifty feet of rope. I say, "Do not worry! I have fifty feet of thread. We can tie my thread to your rope and then tie that to trees on either cliff, then you can go across." You decline my offer and I respond, "What is the matter? Don't you trust the rope?" "Yes," you say, "I trust the rope but I do not trust the thread."

Then let's change the story and make it ninety feet of rope and only ten feet of thread. You're still not comfortable. Then suppose we make it ninety-nine feet of rope and only one foot of thread...one inch of thread? You see, if you have one inch of thread, you will be just as dead on the rocks below as if you tried to cross on a hundred feet of thread. (Kennedy, 1996)

Such is the nature of trust. It connects us; it allows us to go places we could not have gone on our own, and yet, it must be solid or tragedy and doubt can break the connection or divert our paths. In the story above, the thread could be that part of a relationship in which someone is not fully committed, or perhaps he is willing to help, but is not able.

I may see the thread for what it is, and never put my full weight into the relationship, just so that I do not break the connection. I could leave the relationship and go for more rope, hoping the other person would still be there when I returned. Or perhaps, I might let the thread and my rope just stay there without any intention of using it, like an acquaintance friended on Facebook. Or maybe, I could communicate with the other person and let him know that I see the thread and need rope instead. He might have some rope, or know someone who does. Regardless, we would know right away if this relationship could serve its intended purpose, or not, and we could both be better for knowing it.

The next time we meet, I could have a hole torn in my jacket and the same person could offer a thread to fix it. Now the offer is beneficial. At least he did not offer a rope to sew my jacket! It is by our straightforward, honest communication and our openness to hear and be heard that we develop more trust, even if it started off with a thread.

Trust is foundational to all positive human interaction. Join in this journey to discover, or rediscover, when to offer thread to mend our torn coverings or a rope to climb to new heights.

"We're never so vulnerable than when we trust someone - but paradoxically, if we cannot trust, neither can we find love or joy."
                          - Walter Anderson

Situational Trust Model

How do you know if you can trust someone? What is trust anyway? There are many ways to look at the issue of trust and this simple model can help you know how to develop trust with others and determine what you can do to help heal a relationship that is not as strong as it should be.

The situational trust model defines trust with three factors: **ability**, **willingness**, and **intensity** or "risk."

Ability means someone can do what he or she needs to do to get something done. While this is a very broad definition, it serves well to explain the ability factor and how it is used. For example, if I asked someone to show me how to do a certain math problem, they would either have the ability to do it or not. If I ask someone to load a heavy box into my truck, they would either be able to do it or they wouldn't. The ability factor is evaluated by something a person does. The evaluation of this person's ability may be direct (They lift the box.) or made more indirectly. (I walked inside and when I came back out the box was in the truck.)

The willingness factor is similarly general. **Willingness** is based on a person's <u>desire</u> to do something. It does not, however, mean they can do the task. Willingness also implies that the person "wants to" do something for my benefit, even over his or her own desires. If I asked someone to show me how to do a certain math problem, he might be able to do it, but is unwilling. Perhaps we are in a contest for grades and the person is unwilling to help me "get ahead." The person I ask to help load a box into my truck may be willing to help me, however, they might not be able because of a back problem or they are simply too weak.

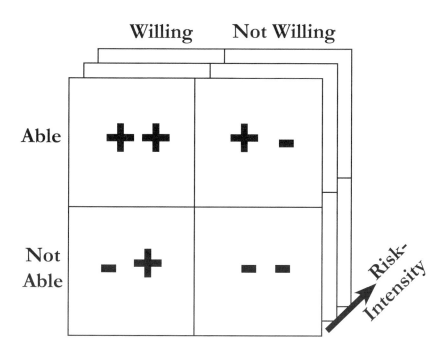

In every interaction these two factors can be used to evaluate if I can trust a person in a particular situation.

I often illustrate the model after doing an activity such as a trust fall. A trust fall is a higher risk activity sometimes used in experiential training where a person falls backwards from an elevated location into the arms of several people below. After doing the trust falls I ask how the participants experienced people's ability and willingness to catch and be caught. Then, I roll out a what-if scenario.

What if the catchers were part of a professional football team. Would you trust them to catch you? But what if they were making jokes and being very distracted by the cheerleaders? They would have the ability to catch you, but not the willingness. Would you trust them?

What if you were standing up high about to fall backwards, the catchers were following all the instructions, focused, and even giving words of encouragement to you. Would you trust them? But what if the catchers were all two-year olds. Would you trust them? They would have the willingness to catch you, but not the ability. And what if your catchers were both unwilling and unable to catch you? You would be a fool to risk yourself by falling into their arms. (Refer to The Punctured Bag activity on page 61.)

> In every interaction these two factors can be used to evaluate whether or not I can trust a person in a particular situation.

The Quadrants

(++) If I believe a person is willing and able to do something I will be able to trust them. If I ask them to do a task or help me in some way and they are successful, it increases my trust in them.

(+ -) Next we have someone who is able but not willing to do something. In this case you know someone can do something because they have demonstrated it before, but for some reason they do not want to do it, so they are unwilling.

(- +) Going to the bottom left quadrant of the model we have a situation that someone is willing to do something, but is unable. Perhaps they are in a new job or situation and want to be helpful, but they still don't know what to do.

(- -) Finally, the remaining quadrant indicates a person who neither is able nor willing to do something. This can be a tough situation when you want to develop trust with someone.

In all four quadrants it is easy to think of examples of tasks people might be doing for you or with you, but the model also helps us simplify strategies for handling relationship issues.

Let's take the topic of **respect** and go deeper into each quadrant.

> Trust is something that is increased or decreased with each interaction.

A person in the upper left quadrant (++) is capable of showing you respect and is willing to do it. The question is, "How do we relate to someone in this quadrant?" Since trust is something that is increased or decreased with each interaction, we need to do something to maintain or further improve the relationship with this (++) person. I would suggest you reciprocate the respect. Show you care in words or actions. Do something or you will risk the person slipping into the other quadrants due to your neglect. It is your part in being trustworthy.

Example: It is desirable to be in the (++) quadrant. Ben and Mike had worked together on projects for several years and got along well. What many people didn't know was that Mike was deaf in his right ear. Ben made an intentional effort to always be on Mike's left side when they worked and he "covered" for him when other people asked Mike questions from the right-hand side and pointed out where questions came from when they were speaking to a group. Ben was able to show respect to Mike and he was willing to do what it took even though it was a bit more effort. Ben's actions developed trust. In contrast, Ben could have regularly forgotten Mike's hearing loss or even teased or ridiculed him about it.

Someone in the upper right quadrant (+-) could show you respect. Maybe they have even done it in the past. However, for some reason they are no longer willing to show respect to you. How do we relate to someone in this quadrant? In this case there is no need to educate the person on the behavior of respect, but there is some unanswered reason they are not showing the respect that could grow into a more trusting relationship. You need to find out why they are acting this way. Perhaps you did something to offend them or maybe they are distracted by another situation in their own life. The point is, you don't know what is going on until you ask them questions to find out about their unwillingness.

Example: Jill and John attend the same university and have had some classes together. In the past they have studied together and helped each other, but in their latest shared class, John seems distant and unwilling to even meet to study. He says she can just study on her own. He has better things to do. John has the ability to study with Jill because he has done it in the past, but for some reason he is unwilling. If Jill wants to build trust, she will need to find out what is going on by asking John. In contrast, Jill could just drop John or get angry with him, but to build the trust, she needs to ask him what has made him unwilling to study together.

In the lower left side (-+) of the quadrant we see a person who is willing to respect you, but unable to do it. Maybe the person comes from a different culture or a difficult home life. The person may be honestly trying to show you respect, but is just not succeeding. How do we relate to someone in this quadrant? In this case there is some education and training that should be applied. A role model or mentor can be very helpful to explain and demonstrate the proper ways to show respect.

Example: Bob and Daun met at a friend's house and Bob knew instantly that he had feelings for her. She had beautiful straight black hair and did not look like she came from Bob's part of the country. Bob had several opportunities to see her in casual situations with other friends. Wanting to impress her, Bob made sure to greet her and make an effort to look into her dark brown eyes. Unfortunately, she didn't seem to connect with him, so he thought he would get to know her better by asking about her and her family. He found out she was Native American, but when he started asking questions about her grandparents and great grandparents she seemed to become cold. Even though he was willing to build a relationship and she was too, he kept showing disrespect by asking about dead family members and actively making eye contact that are taboo in her culture. To show her respect, he needed some education about her culture.

The bottom right quadrant (--) describes a person who is unwilling and unable to show respect. How do we relate to someone in this quadrant? I would imagine it is not too difficult to think of someone in your life or a type of person you know of that would fit into this category. This person seems to consistently annoy you. Not only are their actions disrespectful, they seem unwilling to attempt to make things better. In this situation it is important to ask the person some questions to discover what is going on.

Example: Bill is normally easygoing and friendly; however, Robert makes him very uncomfortable every time they are around each other. Robert makes sarcastic comments and seems to "get into everyone's space." People who work around Robert do admit he is a different kind of person, but they seem to be able to overcome his disruptive behavior. Bill could just avoid Robert, but Robert holds a position on the nonprofit leadership committee Bill wants to join. From Bill's perspective, Robert doesn't know how to be respectful and he certainly doesn't seem to want to change. Bill is in a tough situation. Bill is going to need to take the first step if things are going to get better. Robert may be totally unaware how he is coming across to Bill. Bill is going to have to give him feedback when Robert makes him uncomfortable and ask him why he's doing that. Bill may have to politely "educate" Robert by letting him know what he is doing and why it is an issue.

Many years ago, I was involved in a team building program for a human resources department. We did our usual investigation and assessment to find out what they wanted and why they needed team building. The dynamics were unusual for this team because one of their members was not putting in the work that was expected and he was at risk of being fired if he didn't change his ways. People on the team were frustrated because they normally worked well together, but because this one team member wasn't pulling his weight, everyone had to cover for him. We were allotted two full days of training time that we designed to create an environment where everyone on the team could get closer and learn to work better together. We did several experiential activities and had discussions about various issues with the team. To get at the issue of the team member who was slacking, we waited until near the end of the training so that the strength and safety to deal with the issue was at its highest. Sure enough, the discourse went from a general discussion to increasingly more specific examples of how some assignments were not being done at work. All of a sudden, the person (who was really the focus of the entire training session) realized everyone was talking about him. He had not realized he was making such a negative impact on the team and was also failing so miserably at covering it up. Needless to say he was embarrassed, but appreciative of the concern the rest of the team had about him as a person and his importance to the team. He finally shared what was going on. Both his parents had recently died, and he was dealing with their estate and the grief in his family. He hadn't told anyone about what was going on because he didn't want to burden anyone with his personal problems. When the true situation was finally revealed, he was given time off to focus on his family and the rest of the team happily covered for him during his absence. In his case, he was able and willing to do his job in any normal circumstances, but he was unable and unwilling to manage his personal situation and his work life. He could have easily lost his job if it had not been for the true concern and questions from his team.

Training Note:
From a training perspective it is important to give the participants an opportunity to share examples of relationships they have had that fit into these four situations. This model makes it easy to take the next step to form an action plan focused on developing a more trusting relationship with someone each participant identifies. Participants can even identify where an entire team stands and how to proceed.

> **More trust is required as the risk or perceived risk of the situation is increased.**

Intensity Scale
How deep is your trust?
Another important part of the situational trust model is the intensity or "risk" scale. More trust is required as the risk or perceived risk of the situation is increased.

For example, we put our trust in people and things frequently without even thinking much about it. At the surface-level of the trust matrix there is little sense of risk. As we go into deeper and deeper levels of the matrix, our assessment of people's abilities and willingness or our own willingness and abilities may shift away from the upper left quadrant (++). At some point, the relationship shifts from trust to something less. It's at that point that you can begin to work toward deepening your trust relationship with that person.

So I might be fine with asking a stranger to hold my wallet while I do something like wade in the water to retrieve a golf ball, because they would be in eyesight and it would be a short time in a "safe" setting. I might even be okay with a friend wanting to borrow some cash for lunch because they left their money at home, but not to borrow thousands of dollars for a new wardrobe. I would let my wife borrow my credit card or even manage my bank account, but not a stranger or an acquaintance. As the *perceived* risk increases, the need for a deeper trust relationship increases. So if you can't trust a person in the small things, how can you truly trust them in the bigger things?

Some intensity examples:

Hold my house keys while I get something from my pocket
Visit me at my house for a few days
Store my spare keys at your house in case I lose mine
Take care of my house while I am on vacation

Talk to my daughter
Study with my daughter
Date my daughter
Marry my daughter

Attend my workshop
Work along side me
Work for me independently
Work for yourself
Work for a competitor

Personal introductions
Trust leans
Trust falls
Belay someone jumping off
a high pole

Of course, some people might bring up examples that seem to go against the trust-intensity connection such as flying on a plane with a pilot that you don't even know or getting surgery from a doctor you met only briefly. I would say that the perceived risk is still low because of their professional training. However, it would not take much to quickly change your mind if the pilot acted drunk or the doctor seemed sloppy or unclean. The position a person holds or the expertise they have accumulated will have an effect on the amount of trust another person has with them initially, especially if it is in the context of a normally risky situation. (i.e., The person is a specialist and has training and skills beyond yours.) However, if the person's behavior or performance is contrary to the expectations of their position and experience, the trust level that was assumed initially will lose the advantage it had at the start.

To use the intensity scale as a trust building tool you can go through a similar process you did before with the willing and able parts of the model. First decide in what circumstances you could say you are in the first quadrant (++) with a certain person. Now mentally increase the risk much like the examples given previously. Make them as realistic as possible. Continue this process until you find a situation that slips out of the first quadrant with that person. Is it because of their ability or willingness that your trust decreases? It is at the point where the trust level slips that you can begin to work toward developing a deeper trust relationship.

I should note that the assumption at this point is that there is a need or desire for the relationship to develop more deeply. While striving to be in the first quadrant

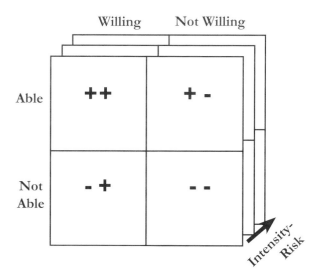

with everyone in all situations might be theoretically ideal, it isn't very practical. Before we shoot for world peace, let's work on developing the relationship with that one particular person as a start.

This model works as a decision matrix for you and your audience. It is especially useful as a tool if people have already been exposed to other models that make use of this matrix strategy of helping people make decisions to take certain actions, such as Situational Leadership (1964) or the Managerial Grid (1985). (See an example of Situational Leadership and Managerial Grid on page 150.) The Situational Trust model is also a good choice if you are focusing on the distinctions between people and tasks, since the "able" component focuses on task skills and the "willingness" component focuses on people skills.

Are they able?

Are they willing?

What's the risk?

How can we move into a (**++**) situation?

"The best way to find out if you can trust somebody is to trust them."
                    – Ernest Hemingway

The Piggy Bank Model

The trust model using the piggy bank is a simple, but powerful way to talk about trust, your actions, reactions, and consequences of behavior. As a facilitator, trainer, or leader, this model is a good choice if you have very limited time and you want to emphasize the importance of each interaction we have with people. The basis of this model comes from Stephen Covey's book, *The 7 Habits of Highly Effective People (*1989).

A Bit of History

During the 1400s in Europe, pottery for house wares was often made with orange clay. Besides plates, bowls and cups, other items that were made with clay were jars, jugs, bottles and containers to hold small items such as loose change. When workers would empty their pockets at the end of the workday, they would empty loose coins or change to put aside for emergency use. This practice may sound very familiar since it is one of the best ways to accumulate quite a sum of money from what we would normally dismiss as trivial. The word "piggy" bank actually derives from the type of clay used for pottery making, which back then was called pygg clay. It wasn't until the 1700s that the word pygg was associated with the hoofed and snouted animal. This happened when a potter made a clay jar in the shape of the pig, which became very appealing in the 20th century. However, in earlier time periods, coins that were collected and saved in the homes were kept in pygg jars; these jars were known as the pygg bank. The earliest examples of coin containers in the shape of pigs have been discovered from the 1300s in Java. (Livious, 2012) The pig was symbolic of prosperity, good fortune, and a connection to the spirits of the soil. It is easy to see why they would form pottery vessels shaped like round-bellied pigs to hold their small coins. Below is the model, an explanation of the model, and a few key points.

So what do we put into piggy banks? Money. What kinds of money? Coins, various, small change goes into it. Rarely do we put large denomination bills or diamond rings into them. It's the same way with relationship trust accounts. We make small deposits into them to build trust with someone. Some deposits may be larger or smaller than others, but it takes time and consistency to accumulate a large amount. In practice, we don't have to save someone's life to get him or her to trust us more. It can be done as simply as opening a door or saying, "Thank you."

The Trust Account
Imagine that all of us have a trust piggy bank that we carry around with us everywhere we go. With each interaction we are either making deposits or withdrawals by our behavior and others' perceptions of those behaviors. Our goal is to increase what is in their bank or at least maintain what is in there. Unfortunately, we aren't perfect and things will happen that cause us to take a withdrawal from time to time. Perhaps I showed up late to a meeting or I said something that was taken as offensive. If their account is large and the withdrawal is small, our trusting relationship is still okay, but if the account is small, even a small withdrawal can be significant. It reminds me of a couple in love. They add to each other's accounts any way they can think of and they are motivated to do so. They trust each other. Then they get married and the accounts may not be as

actively filled. Little annoying habits start to cause tiny withdrawals and eventually an account can become empty. They argue and the trust that was there before seems to have mysteriously disappeared. Without understanding why, the relationship has changed from trust to distrust or disgust. Of course this doesn't have to

happen. The couple could have communicated about the withdrawals before they emptied the bank and they could have been intentional about making deposits. It is true that people are either making deposits or withdrawals all the time. There are no neutral interactions. Even doing nothing will tend to take away from the account, unless perhaps the person makes deposits by stopping doing something that annoys you.

Deposits are those actions and words that add to someone's trust account. (A kind word, helping someone with a task, etc.) They can be as easy as saying, "Please," "Thank you," and "Hello." "That presentation was great!" Be sure to be sincere with your deposits. If people perceive you are flattering them or insincere, your deposits will quickly turn to withdrawals. What are some other specific examples of trust deposits?

Withdrawals are those actions or words that take away from someone's trust account.

Balance is the amount of trust in the relationship. It indicates the sum of the deposits minus the withdrawals.

Bank breakers are behaviors that zero-out a trust account: Lie, Cheat, Steal

Trust Account Exercise
What are ways you can put small deposits into someone's account?

1.

2.

3.

4.

5.

What are examples of small withdrawals you see people take? Be specific.

1.

2.

3.

4.

5.

Sometimes a deposit for one person is a withdrawal for another person (e.g., You praise a girl on her beautiful freckles, but she hates having freckles.) To many girls it would be a nice complement, but to her it is a withdrawal.

Give an example or two of a deposit you can give to someone you know well that might not work well for people in general.

1.

2.

The better we know someone, the better we can make special (valuable) deposits into their account. If you give a gift to a close friend, you can make sure the gift is the person's favorite color, style, or flavor. It can represent an experience you have had together. It can be personal and special.

Of course the withdrawals can cost more too when we know the other person well. Some people know how to "push your buttons" or embarrass you.

Overall, this trust model is useful to make people aware of how to develop trust with people and realize what things they do to negatively have an impact on relationships. If people can be intentional about their interactions, they can make great strides toward developing beneficial habits.

"Anyone who doesn't take truth seriously in small matters cannot be trusted in large ones either."

— Albert Einstein

Behavioral Model of Trust

Another model that can be quite useful, ties four elements of trust to four behavioral styles, preferences, or temperaments. Most of today's four-type assessments are based on the original research done by William Marston in his book, *Emotions of Normal People*. (1928) Examples of these include the DiSC Style Inventory, and the Predictive Index. If you are administering one of the many style inventories available, this model can offer a natural fit into the discussion of trust.

The model consists of four main components to trust and each of the four has two secondary parts to further develop clarity and depth of understanding. The Elements of Trust™ model comes from Intégro Leadership Institute through the development and research of Keith Ayers and Dr. Ralph Colby.

Congruence: "I walk my talk."
Straightforwardness
I ensure people are clear about what is expected of them.
Honesty
Having high standards of honesty in everything I do.

Openness: "I am open to others' ideas and opinions."
Receptivity
Giving ideas and methods a fair hearing.
Disclosure
Communicating openly my own ideas and opinions.

<u>Acceptance</u>: "Who you are is okay with me."
> **Respect**
>> People are valued by me and not put down for whom they are.
>
> **Recognition**
>> I am sure people get the recognition they deserve.

<u>Reliability</u>: "You can count on me."
> **Seeks excellence**
>> Striving to do the best in everything I do.
>
> **Keeps commitments**
>> I follow through on my responsibilities and promises.

Congruence is correlated to those people described as direct, dominant, fast-paced, self-certain, and task oriented.

Openness is related most to people who are outgoing, influential, talkative, and motivational.

Acceptance is related most closely to people described as accommodating, stabilizing, steady, loyal, easygoing, and patient.

Reliability is most related to people who are logical, conscientious, analytical, consistent, and perfectionist.

In each of the trust elements, a person's natural behavioral style will tend to make him or her more likely to be strong in that area. For example, someone who is direct and self-certain will tend to be straightforward in their interactions and will likely value that straightforwardness from others too when developing trust.

If someone is strong in all four elements of the model, people should perceive him or her as very trustworthy. Of course each of us has certain parts of this trust model we accomplish better than others. It will be important to communicate to people that they should first recognize and fully use the strengths they have naturally, then work to strengthen those areas in which they struggle if they want to develop more trusting relationships.

For example, I naturally excel in the areas of reliability and acceptance. People can count on me to show up to meetings on time, fulfill my promises, and go into relationships really listening and accepting them for what they bring to the table. However, people realize as they get to know me, that I keep a majority of opinions and comments to myself. There is a lot more happening inside my head than I share. That can cause people to lose some trust in me because I am being closed and private. I also avoid confrontation whenever I can, so being up front and straightforward is difficult for me. I do work on speaking up and saying what is on my mind, but it is something I have to do deliberately. For day-to-day interactions I can sometimes enlist the strengths of others. My wife, for example, has no problem confronting a salesclerk if something is wrong or negotiating a hotel rate. She is happy to use her strengths, and I am happy to let her. Overall as a family, others can learn to trust us more because we excel at three of the four areas and we intentionally work to be more open.

Based on the results of a number of behavioral assessments, people can learn what strengths they tend to have related to trust and what they are likely to value most from other people. They can also realize what behavior may not come so easily and have an action plan to be more intentional with that type of behavior so that it strengthens their trustworthiness. It is by the behavior we exhibit that people can start to trust us, not by our intentions alone.

Also notice that Congruence and Reliability are based on the <u>tasks</u> we do with other people to determine trust while Openness and Acceptance are based on the <u>relationship</u> we develop with others that then leads to trust. The first is focused on developing or testing for a trustworthy relationship while the second is developing a relationship to then determine if someone is worthy of our trust.

(Trust then Relationship? or Relationship then Trust?)

What are your natural strengths to develop trust?

What types of behavior do you need to practice more if you want to broaden and improve your trust and trustworthiness?

Leadership Trust Model

This model for developing trust can be used from two perspectives:
• training and facilitating leaders
• improving your own relationships with the participants in your classes or programs.

If you are focused on training leaders and want to address some powerful aspects to increase trust between leaders and followers, this is a very direct model to introduce. If you want to improve your own trustworthiness with the participants in your programs, this may offer some ideas to do just that. (Imagine, a trainer or facilitator using his or her own material to improve!)

Trust is a psychological state in which one party is willing, "to be vulnerable to the actions of another party based on the expectation that the other will perform a particular action important to the trustor" (Mayer, Davis, & Schoorman, 1995, p. 712)

The model for leadership trust consists of four factors: Ability, benevolence, integrity, and propensity to trust. The first three factors are the responsibility of the leader and the last factor is dependent on the people or person who is being led. The four factors are listed in order of strength and may be used for building trust between a leader and followers, boss and employees, teacher and students, facilitator/trainer and participants, etc. The model also graphically shows that "ability" is approximately as important as both "benevolence" and "integrity" combined while "propensity to trust" is

significantly smaller.

Ability - A leader's capacity to accomplish tasks required of the employer and employee relationship and to demonstrate relevant skills and competencies.

Benevolence - Being other-focused, employees and followers will not trust a leader who appears overly concerned with his or her own interests.

Integrity - A leader is true to his or her convictions and has a reputation of honest encounters with others.

Propensity to trust - Some individuals are generally more likely to initiate trust than others. It is a characteristic of the trustor.

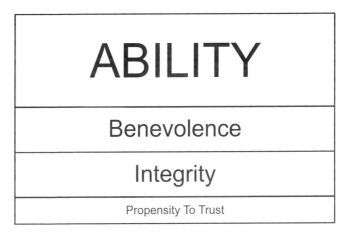

For many years there have been studies focused on what makes a program or an event a success. Consistently it is revealed that the leader and facilitator make the biggest difference, even more than money and other tangible and technical resources. (Schuman, 1996)

Leaders and facilitators are highly influential in the outcome of programs. Therefore, it is important that a leader develop trusting relationships so that people can be positively influenced and work together with a focus on their mission rather than one eye on the task and another on the leader and the other people for whom they lack trust.

At the beginning of any class or gathering there is an awkwardness that can be overcome more quickly by the leader through practicing behavior such as learning names and making eye contact, using direct body positioning, displaying confidence, using head nods, dressing informally, and the like. By practicing such behavior that reportedly reduces barriers and increases psychological closeness between a leader, facilitator, or teacher and participants, they can influence a positive effect among people and thereby influence the group's achievement and participation.

What does ability mean?

Initially, it seems that most people think of ability in terms of "hard" skills. Can the leader of the kitchen cook? Does the chemistry professor know what will happen when we heat that beaker of chemicals? Can the river guide read the water and direct us down the rapids? The hard skills needed to do the job are important, especially when the people being led are vulnerable to any accidents or hardships. A mountain guide needs to know the path and the weather so that people are not stranded or hurt. Lawyers have to know the laws and be able to create documents that will serve as binding agreements. But there is another aspect of ability that is just as important, dependent on the setting. A leader (trainer, teacher, facilitator, guide, boss) also needs the ability to use "soft" skills. Soft skills are people and relationship skills as simple as smiling and as difficult as calming an angry group. For many leaders, the soft skills are the more difficult. Part of the reason for the difficulty is that people are complex and often unpredictable. Even physical gestures, a tone of voice, the experiences of the leader, the experiences of the audience, and timing all play into a leader's ability to develop trust. Therefore, ability means a leader can do their tasks and work with people. If leadership is about influencing people, people skills are one of the tasks of leaders.

What is benevolence?

Like other trust models, this one favors a person who is not selfish. Benevolence means focused on the good of others. I don't exist as a leader to help myself and bring attention to myself. I am here to help other people shine and do more than they ever thought possible. If a leader does benevolence well, his or her success comes from the results of the people they lead. Small statements can signal to the group you are working with whether or not you are benevolent. "Let's get this done so I can make it to the golf course on time," is not sending a good message. What are some common benevolence squashing statements you can think of?

On the other hand, encouraging the group and giving them the credit like saying a sincere, "You did it!" or "Congratulations on doing such a great job," will help communicate that you have their best interests in mind.

Integrity?

The most common definition I hear for integrity is, "Doing the right thing, even when no one is watching you." Furthermore, what you do and what you say are in alignment. Honesty about whom you are and what you believe in, even when it is not popular, demonstrates your integrity.

Losing your integrity can occur subtly. You can say you will meet a deadline or reach a goal then change your mind. You can say you will hold a group to a certain standard, then compromise because they came very close to reaching their goal. Sometimes leaders play "favorites" with participants when the standards are supposed to be equally applied. In all cases, integrity is about holding to the truth and to the standards you have established through your words or actions.

It is a curious finding that benevolence and integrity posted such similar relative impacts on trust in the research. Given that integrity was about how the leader treated others and benevolence was about how the leader directly treated a participant, this finding suggests that participants may place considerable emphasis on information they gather regarding the leader's behavior toward other group members as well as how the leader responds to them as individuals. Taken together, the success of these two variables supports the notion that a leader's character is important to participants (Hobbs & Ewert, 2008).

> In all cases, integrity is about holding to the truth and to the standards you have established through your words or actions.

Propensity to trust?

Some people have an easier time trusting than others. Why are people this way? Facilitating many teams over the years, I have often asked for answers to that question and the responses ultimately fall into two categories: personality and experiences. Some personality traits tend to welcome relationships enthusiastically while others are more guarded and skeptical. And experiences for some people have been nurturing and supportive while others have been harsh or even abusive.

Are you the kind a person who tends to put your trust in people until they prove to you they are untrustworthy? Or, are you the kind of person whose trust has to be earned from the beginning of any relationship. Neither one of these types of people is necessarily wrong in their approach to trust; yet both types tend to be in every group, classroom, or business. From a leader's perspective, a person's propensity to trust is up to the trustor, yet it is still important to be aware that no matter how able, benevolent, and honest the leader is, there are still opportunities for surprises, both good and bad. Some people will tend to trust and demonstrate trust in you, while others will not be so readily vulnerable to your actions as a leader. In other words, even if your trustworthiness as a leader is near perfect, some people still will not put their trust in you, at least not at first.

Training Note:
In the research focused on outdoor leaders and the participants they lead, there was only a small statistical impact regarding the propensity to trust and the ultimate trust in the leader, yet it is still worth noting. I know that there have been participants in my trainings that came in with "baggage" from their past. One in particular attended a team building program and was highly skeptical of me and the whole idea of experiential training. It turned out that this person had experienced another training in which all the participants were treated like little kids and the activities that the leader used

embarrassed this person. Fortunately, over the course of the training, he realized our training was focused on his work team and designed appropriately for the professionals that they were. So in response to the research findings, I think the impact of the propensity to trust is a function of time and experience with the new leader. Some people are more hesitant to trust at first, but can be influenced by proof of trustworthiness over time.

How competent are you at your position? In what ways do you demonstrate it?

How do you "prove" benevolence to others by your behavior?

What is an example of you demonstrating your integrity when it could have easily gone another way?

What is your propensity to trust? (I trust you until you break trust. You have to prove you are worthy of my trust.)

> Truly human leadership protects an organization from the internal rivalries that can shatter a culture. When we have to protect ourselves from each other, the whole organization suffers. But when trust and cooperation thrive internally, we pull together and the organization grows stronger as a result.
> — Simon Sikek, Leaders Eat Last

Advice for the Trainer and Facilitator

The trainer or facilitator for a group of people has an awesome responsibility, especially if the topic is focused on trust. The following section includes some of the most important information and advice for creating a trusting environment I have discovered.

Before The Event

It was about 15 minutes before I was scheduled to work with a group of over 100 educators. I had finished organizing everything so I decided to sit in the middle of one of the rows of chairs to make sure people would be able to see the projection screen. While I was sitting there relaxing for a moment, some people started showing up and sitting down. One woman sat near me on the same row where I was sitting, so I decided to have a bit of fun. "Hi, how are you?" I asked. "I'm doing all right," she said. "What are you here for?" I asked. "I'm here to learn some things I can use with my students," she said. "What have you heard about this guy who's presenting?" I asked hoping for something that would not embarrass either one of us. "I don't really know, but I have heard it should be fun," she said. "I hope it's good too," I said as I got up and excused myself. After talking to several other people in the room I headed to the microphone and welcomed everyone. The look on the woman's face was priceless. Since that first time of being a little mischievous, I continue to realize the value of talking with people who will be participating just before the event begins. It does not come naturally. My natural instinct would have me focus on lists of details and stay hidden until I was "on." However, I now know that I can use my nervous energy to get to know a few people and find out people's moods and hopes for the presentation. Then when the program is in progress, I already have some "friends" in the audience and possibly an interesting new story to share. From the audience's perspective it also makes me "human" and not like someone from another world very different from theirs.

Preparation

Know what you are going to say before you say it. That does not mean is has to be scripted or memorized word for word, but know in your mind what you will do and say first, second, etc. Having a schedule or some notes to look at is not only fine, but it is a good idea. However, it is best that you look through your notes while the group in engaged in activity rather than while they are focused on you.

The Learning Environment

If you want people to develop new trust skills, they will need to be in a space where they can hear and be heard. Minimize distractions especially from people outside the group. Today with all the technology around us, it is a good idea to request phones to not be used and recording to not be allowed. If someone believes they are being recorded, meaningful interaction and discussion will suffer.

When it is practical, set all the chairs in a circle with any tables on the outside of the circle. It might be a little awkward for some people at first, but it will greatly enhance the interaction. When training facilitators, I will often set the room with a circle of chairs and one empty chair in the center of the circle to demonstrate how important the room setting is. I sit in one of the chairs in the circle. As people come into the room, it is interesting to hear their comments and questions about that center chair and watch how many people pay more attention to that chair. There is often a noticeable stress level and many assumptions made about why that chair is empty and in the middle of the circle. When the session starts, I immediately discuss the chair, make any relevant points, then remove it from the center. Often people say they assumed the center chair was a punishment for the last person who arrived. Others assume their will be some sort of exercise that "puts them on the spot' or in the "firing line." The lesson is that even small things, like chair placement, decorations, what you wear, etc., can have a significant impact.

With larger groups, sit them at round tables whenever possible. At least then, everyone can interact easily with people at their table and you can move around easily from table to table.

Build Confidence and Trust
There is a saying, "Never let them see you sweat." There is a lot of wisdom in that saying. If you want people to have confidence in your presentation, you need to show the confidence by your behavior. If you want people to trust that you have something wonderful in store for them, you need to show them you are trustworthy. It is rare for a presenter to be totally confident and relaxed, but if you look the part, you will soon be more confident and relaxed because of how the group is responding to you. It is a process of going from new and unstable when you first start, to experienced and stable as people get more

familiar and comfortable. Trust the process.

On the other hand, be sure to be genuine in your efforts to show confidence. If you tend to be quiet and shy, a burst of false enthusiasm will not go well. Consider instead, increasing your volume slightly and talking to people more while you make eye contact. People can detect when you are overacting or creating a facade and that decreases trust. In the end, nothing beats preparation and practice to project confidence.

Sequence Your Training
Like any good book or movie, your presentation needs a beginning, middle, and an end. It is not about entertaining them, but rather about beginning the journey at the beginning and finishing when the goals of the training are fulfilled. I like to think of sequencing like a set of stairs to climb. You start the group at the bottom with topics and fairly simple activities that help them become acquainted. For each step up the stairs, you will be adding to the perceived risk and complexity of the activities or topics while always making sure it helps the people develop and grow closer to their goals.

A common phrase I use is, "Teach, Test, Progress." First, you present some information, then you test to see if they understand what you presented (usually through an activity), and if they "pass the test," you progress by taking another step up the stairs. If they don't seem to understand what you presented and don't "pass the test," then present the information in a different way. In the past, I have used this sequencing strategy to keep people physically safe when they were learning commands, doing trust leans, then trust falls. It works well even when you are focused on relationship trust instead of physical trust. Hurt feelings and harsh words can be just as damaging as falling down.

The fundamental importance of trust development is well recognized. "Faith and trust in self and the other person is such an essential ingredient in relationships that it cuts across and interacts with all other components..." of the self-concept system. (Fits, p. 15). Erik Erikson's eight stages of human development place the establishment of trust as the first basic task of life development. (See the eight stages on page 151.) Each successive "Identity Stage" of a person's life is formed on the basis of this ability to trust. Without trust there is no "glue" to hold relationships together. The beauty of the sequencing of trust activities is that there is a built-in rationale for the group to "practice" trust before moving on to the next activity as well as throughout the process. Trust is the key to personal involvement.

Behavior of the Trainees
Similar to setting a safe physical environment, it is important to set some expectations of people's behavior too. A common response to fear or anxiety in a group is sarcasm or "dark humor." An example of dark humor might sound like, "Don't worry about speaking your mind; they haven't fired anyone in months for that." Discourage dark humor because it causes doubt and mistrust. As a part of some experiential activities, there are "afflictions" that occur if someone steps off something they are balanced on or touches something they are supposed to avoid. Afflictions serve to counteract a mistake or be a form of correction for doing something incorrectly. They are fabricated by the facilitator and usually include things

like loss of eyesight, inability to speak, or inability to use an arm or leg. One of these afflictions I use is called contra language. The person who gets the affliction is informed that now everything he or she says must be the opposite of what he or she really means. Up is down, right is left, good is bad, etc. If the person likes to talk, they will say the opposite, as they are supposed to, but sometimes they start saying what they are actually meaning. At that point, the team will tend to ignore whatever they say, because now people are confused about whether the person's words are intentionally honest or intentionally dishonest. Dark humor does the same thing. People become confused and untrusting because they don't know what is truly meant by the words. Is it an attempt at humor, or is it a jab? Instead, ask people to be respectful of each other. Encourage and even challenge people to use supportive language and words that will inspire confidence. We prove we are trustworthy to a person when they are vulnerable or are at risk and we come through for them in a positive way. We should provide an arena for people to prove themselves trustworthy.

Activities of Trust
Every activity dealing with trust has a risk that the participant feels vulnerable to. Some risks are real and some risks are perceived but unfounded. Nevertheless, a person still feels vulnerable. For the purposes of training, I personally prefer activities that have high-perceived risks and low actual risks. A couple of activities that come to mind are Mousetrap Trust Sequence (See page 82.) and William Tell (See page 90.). Each of those seems dangerous and even crazy to some people. Actually having people put their hands onto a loaded

mousetrap or intentionally shoot a rubber band toward someone's head can seem too extreme. However, the actual risks are very small. Someone could chip a fingernail, but they won't lose a finger or break a bone to a mousetrap. Someone could be hit in the face with a rubber band, but with eye protection, injury just doesn't happen. With some of the relationship activities such as You Betcha (See page 117.), people can get temporarily angry or upset, but it is a contrived situation that helps people understand how we humans behave when we are in certain circumstances and the only real consequence is losing to another team in the activity. I would rather have people experience success or failure in a safe environment than to jump into real situations on the very first attempt. If given the opportunity, who wouldn't want to build skills and confidence in a safe setting, then tackle real situations that are important? It goes back to sequencing. Resolving actual trust issues comes later, after a strong foundation of trust and strategies to improve trust have been developed.

Allow People to Choose to Participate
People will trust and respect you as a trainer if you avoid forcing them into something they do not want to do or rigidly expecting them to participate in one certain way. The following "philosophy" is how I frame participation in my training and it works very well.

"**Challenge By Discovery**" is the philosophy by which we operate the training.

You will be presented with many different situations and challenges. How you participate is up to you as long as it is done safely. You aren't going to be forced into doing anything. It's your choice. A goal of the training is for you to get involved in such a way that you can discover what works and what doesn't work for you and those around you. Most of the activities we do involve working with others.

Pay attention to what you are doing and what others are doing and we will discuss how effective it is and what (if anything) can be improved. Your ongoing challenge will be to take the risk to discover something new and useful about yourself and those you work with.

Givens:
• We are each unique and because of that, our actions and strategies to accomplish things will not be identical to those of other people. Our actions in teams will also be unique. That is why team building is so important to do with every team.

• Truth is discovered...not created, believed, or wished into existence.

• There are many ways to accomplish things; however, the "better" or "best" ways are worth the effort to discover.

• People learn to do things by doing them. A person can see pictures, hear lectures, and be taught about a particular subject, but until they do it, they have just learned about it.

Control and Trust

Many people, from the time they were little kids, have been told, "Stay in control; don't get out of control." During training I have heard participants sincerely say, "I trust these people, but I can't seem to do this activity." The issue was more about losing control than trust. In trust activities the participants are putting themselves in a "risky" situation - relying on the emotional and sometimes physical support of the group. This "letting go of control" requires patience, practice, progression, and safety. This looks and feels different for everyone. Unfortunately, the need to be in control, if it is a reoccurring issue, can have a negative effect on others' trust of the person wanting to maintain control.

> The issue was more about losing control than trust.

If someone is having trouble being trusted because they need to be in control of everything, they need to strive for more of a balance for them to be more effective. As a facilitator, you should consider how you might provide a variety of levels or opportunities to experience and practice trust. Be prepared to offer alternatives or variations. For example, if it is a physical trust issue about falling into a team's arms, try simply leaning past the point of balance. If it is a relationship trust issue like being straightforward giving feedback in the group, perhaps the person could do it one-on-one or in writing.

One More Thought

Above all, remember some basic wisdom: <u>communicate to your audience</u>. Meet them where they are, based on factors such as their age, their affiliation, their expectations, their culture, and their setting. I might have the same topic for a group of kids at camp and an audience of engineers in a hotel, but it will not work well if I present to both groups in the same way. Instead, use two trust fundamentals: speak their language and show you desire the best for them.

Who is my audience?
(youth, adults, salespeople, leaders, engineers, etc.)

What is the goal?
(have fun, get to know each other, resolve conflicts, etc.)

How do they tend to communicate?
(low-tech, high-tech, in groups, one-on-one, etc.)

The glory of friendship is not the outstretched hand, nor the kindly smile, nor the joy of companionship; it's the spiritual inspiration that comes to one when he discovers that someone else believes in him and is willing to trust him with his friendship.
                    - Ralph Waldo Emerson

Experiential Learning Activities

Experiential learning is, basically, learning by doing. It is through activity and discussions of the activity that people truly realize what works and what doesn't. When people already know how to be most effective, the experiences give them an opportunity to practice their skills.

Experience-based training is an approach to learning used to develop relationships, enhance performance, or influence organization-wide improvements. Experiential training typically includes action, reflection, discussion, transfer, and support for individuals or groups of learners.

Experience-based training is one of the most effective tools for facilitating organizational and personal improvement. It consists of some traditional training methods blended with activities that bring out the "people dynamics" in situations. It can be focused on specific outcomes and is led by practitioners able to help your organization, your leaders, or your people make tangible and meaningful transfers between a learning experience and ongoing real-world challenges.

The thirteen activities on the following pages are focused on trust and trustworthiness. However, the emphasis of the activities is on relationship trust rather than physical trust. Because of this, there are no activities that require catching people or wearing blindfolds. Those activities can be very valuable, but are outside the scope of this book.

"To see far is one thing; going there is another."
                                        - Constantin Brancusi

Matrix Of Recommended Team Sizes For Activities

Number In Team	2-5	6-10	11-15	16-20	21-30	31+	Time
Paper Folding	•	•	•	•	•	•	15
Indian Numbers	•	•	•	•			15
The Punctured Bag	•	•	•	•	•	•	15
Trustworthiness Ranking *	•	•					30
Photo Finish		•	•	•			30
Mousetrap Trust Sequence *	•						30
Faith Walk		•	•	•	•		30
William Tell *	•						30
Cutthroat Raptor *	•	•					60
Hanging By A Thread *		•					60-90
Win As Much As You Can *	•	•					60
You Betcha *	•	•					60
Community Chest *	•	•					60

When referring to the team size matrix, anytime you see the "*" remember that the recommended team size does not mean the total number of participants in your group, but how many per team in the activity. For example, the Mousetrap Trust Sequence has teams of two or three, yet you may have more than a hundred people doing the activity at once.

The times, in minutes, are approximate and include some discussion time after the activity.

Paper Folding

PROPS:
• 1 sheet of 8.5 x 11 copy paper - You as a presenter can have the only sheet or you may also distribute a sheet to small groups of 2-4 people.

OBJECTIVE:
Demonstrate what happens to someone who loses trust and whose trust is restored

HISTORY:
I was listening to a radio program on my way to facilitate

a team building session and the host was saying that a sheet of paper could not be folded in half more than seven times. Thinking it through in my head, the visual struck me as a great way to explain the consequences of losing trust.

INSTRUCTIONS:
After discussing what trust is, hold up a sheet of plain paper and ask the group to imagine it represents a person.

Ask them to describe this person. (e.g., flat, no marks, smooth, perfect, regular, etc.)

Then ask for people to give examples of things that break or decrease trust. (e.g., say harsh words, be mean, push,

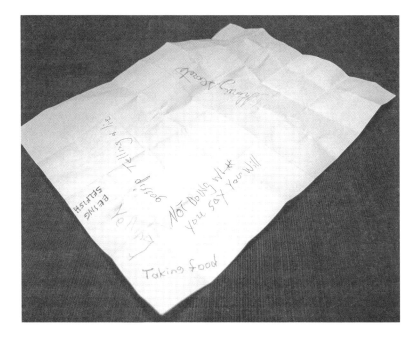

lie, share secrets, etc.) After each example the group says, fold the paper in half. You will likely have to stop folding after the sixth example because the paper will be too small and hard to fold.

Ask the group to describe this "person" now that all these trust breakers have happened. (e.g., they are closed, damaged, rigid, never be the same, etc.)

Then challenge them to describe what they would need to do to develop or regain trust with this person. (e.g., be their friend, apologize, spend time with them, etc.) After each example of a trust builder, unfold the paper. Continue asking for examples until the paper is completely unfolded. Then congratulate the group for restoring this "person's" trust and ask them to describe this person now. (e.g., open but wrinkled, damaged, never quite the same, etc.) How is this paper like a real person's relationship?

At this point, you can emphasize another truth about people and trust relationships by asking what would happen if this "person's" trust was broken again. At this point you can fold the paper back to its smallest size (even with one hand) to make the point that it is much easier now for this "person" to return to a closed position, much the same way that some people have a predisposition not to trust certain types of people or situations. They have already been "bent" that way.

FACILITATOR NOTES:
This is a quick and easy demonstration activity. Some groups seem to have an easier time thinking of various ways to destroy trust than to increase or restore trust. I

usually point out that there is probably a lesson there.

If you plan to refold the paper at the end, practice a few times before you present it in a group setting. By the looks on some people's faces, I can tell it makes a strong point if you can quickly fold it back to its smallest size with one hand.

VARIATIONS:
• Ask small groups to write their negative "lose trust" examples on their paper as they fold it, then write positive "trust enhancing" examples as they unfold it.

• Use a flip chart sheet of paper and often get up to seven folds.

POTENTIAL DISCUSSION QUESTIONS:
• What are ways you can keep an open and honest relationship?

• What are some examples of the easiest way to "fold" you (lose your trust)?

• If you were a sheet of paper, how would you look today?

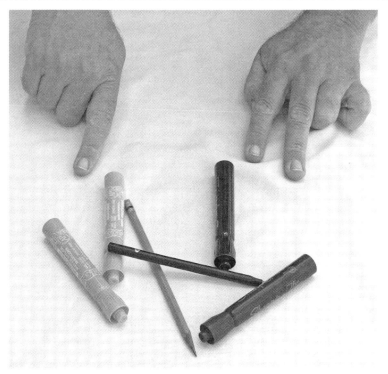

Indian Numbers

PROPS:
• 4 or 5 pens, sticks, or other small objects

OBJECTIVE:
To identify what number the facilitator is showing. Also to teach that we may not see obvious things unless we are looking for them, such as behavior that develops or reduces trust.

HISTORY:
This activity is a very old classic. Typically people are introduced to it at a camp because the facilitator needs to fill some time. It is intended to misdirect the participants

until people understand what they are looking for.

PREPARATION:
Find a location where everyone can see in front of you and you have a comfortable place to sit. It may be at a table or on the floor.

INSTRUCTIONS:
I am going to arrange a few objects in front of me. Your challenge is to identify what number I am making. It will be anything from a 0 to a 10. When you have figured out how to identify the numbers, keep quiet about it and let others discover the solution for themselves.

(Place the four or five objects in some pattern and ask if anyone knows what number it is. At the same time, place your hands on the table or floor near your body and show with your fingers a number 0 through 10. The point is that they should be looking at the objects, not your hands. So don't draw attention to your hands.)

What number is it? (Most of the time someone will take a guess. If it's right, congratulate them, if it's wrong, let them know what it was then rearrange the objects and show a new number. Continue showing different numbers until people start realizing you are simply showing the number by your fingers and the objects are just a distraction. For some groups, it may take several rounds before they figure it out.)

FACILITATOR NOTES:
This activity can be frustrating for some people. Be encouraging and offer several opportunities to guess different numbers. If a group is struggling for a while, feel

free to slowly show clues. Clues might include: arranging the objects in the same pattern, but they "represent" a different number or placing your hands closer and closer to the objects each time you make a new number. At times, I have had to place my hands on top of the objects before people understood that they should be looking at my fingers for answers. Don't laugh; I'm sure we all experience the same thing in real life before we understand some things.

POTENTIAL DISCUSSION QUESTIONS:
• What made this activity difficult?

• For those first few people who figured it out, how did you do it?

• Who here has ever been confused by someone's reaction to a situation?

• How could this activity help you understand what might be going on?

• Some people say they find it difficult to see trust and distrust. How might you "open your eyes" to what is really going on?

"Those who trust us educate us."
     - T. S. Eliot

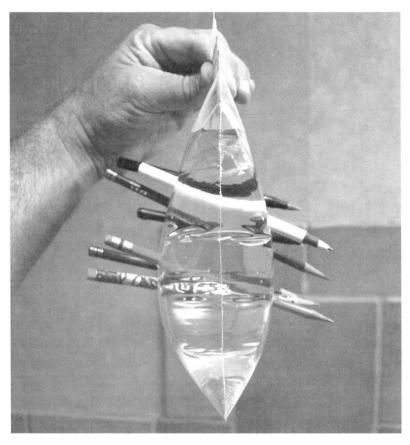

The Punctured Bag

PROPS:
• A pint or quart-sized resealable plastic bag
• Pens or pencils
• Water

OBJECTIVE:
Stick pens and pencils through a bag of water to teach risk taking and commonsense trust.

HISTORY:

I was introduced to this demonstration activity many years ago. It was actually presented as a party game, no doubt, to trick some poor victim into an embarrassing situation.

PREPARATION:

The presenter fills a resealable pint or quart-sized plastic bag with water and has a few sharpened pencils handy. A "brave" volunteer is asked to be part of a magic trick by sitting in a chair in the middle of the room while the presenter holds the bag of water over the volunteer's

head.

INSTRUCTIONS:

The presenter asks, "Do you trust me?" The person usually says, "Yes."

Addressing everyone in the room, the presenter asks, "What do you predict will happen when I poke this pencil into this water-filled bag?" Skeptical answers typically range from "it will pop," to "the water will run out."

"Well, there's one way to find out," says the presenter as he drives the pencil horizontally through both sides of the bag so that the point is sticking out on one side and the eraser is sticking out the other side. If he has done it right, there isn't even a drop of water that comes out.

"Maybe I just got lucky," he says, now driving two or three more pencils through the bag one at a time. If he's been careful, there won't be any spillage.

"Now do you trust me?" he asks the volunteer. Usually the volunteer answers affirmatively. "So would you trust me to remove the pencils while holding the bag over your head?" Sometimes the volunteer says yes and the presenter asks for a prediction from the audience. If the volunteer says no, then the presenter asks for another volunteer to take his place in the chair. Usually someone will.

"So I am going to remove the pencils. How confident are you that this is going to turn out well?" The person sitting in the chair is typically nervous, but confident everything will be all right. So the presenter quickly pulls out one or more of the pencils and water starts streaming out both sides of the bag. If the presenter wants to be nice, most of the liquid will actually miss the volunteer because it squirts out to the sides. However, if the presenter is not as kind, the bag can be moved to aim the water directly onto the volunteer, soaking him and embarrassing him for a laugh.

FACILITATOR NOTES:
One of the lessons in trust from this activity is the way the presenter creates a seemingly risky situation (poking the bag and possibly soaking the volunteer), but accomplishes the task without getting the volunteer wet. The volunteer was vulnerable, but the presenter succeeded in keeping the volunteer safe. It is a simple physics application using the pencil to create two holes, but at the same time plug them like a stopper in a sink because the plastic hugs the pencil and doesn't rip. If the presenter had stopped at that point in the demonstration, he might have actually increased trust with the volunteer and the audience.

However, since the presenter went to the next step of pulling the pencils out of the bag and the holes couldn't "heal" themselves, water ran out. Common sense would say that the water was going to spill out, but the influence of the presenter overcame rational thought. At that point, the presenter likely lost the trust of the people and taught them to be skeptical of the presenter, possibly any presenter in the future too. No one likes to be tricked.

If you decide to stop after putting the pencils into the bag, start a discussion about what would happen when the pencils were removed. After the discussion, pull out the pencils and let people see what really happens. This can be a teachable moment illustrating the circumstances people get into when they go too far and suffer from poor decisions such as doing drugs, stealing, trusting untrustworthy people, etc.

POTENTIAL DISCUSSION QUESTIONS:

• Tell us about your thoughts and feelings when I was starting the activity.

• What was it that influenced someone to sit in a chair and allow a bag of water to speared overhead?

• What was it that made someone willing to sit below the bag when I pulled the pens out?

• How can you discern when to trust and when not to trust?

"Trusting too much to others' care is the ruin of many."
— Benjamin Franklin

Trustworthiness Ranking

PROPS:
• Paper (optional)
• Pens or pencils (optional)

OBJECTIVE:
Discover what you value the most when it comes to trust.

PREPARATION:
Make sure the people in the group know each other well enough to have some opinion of who people are and how they behave. Doing a few experiential activities ahead of time works well even though they might have started as strangers.

INSTRUCTIONS:
Divide the whole group into small groups of 5-7 people.

Ask the small groups to sit in a circle and honestly evaluate each person in the circle over the next 5 minutes. You are asking each team member to secretly rank order the people in their circle from most trustworthy to least trustworthy. In addition to rank ordering the people, ask them to write down or simply keep in mind what characteristics made one person rank higher than another. To make this task easier, it is often best to determine who is most trustworthy, then who is least trustworthy, then work on the people in the middle of the ranking.

After the 5 minutes of silence, we will be discussing what you discovered, but we will <u>not</u> be asking you to reveal your rankings.

The Rules:
1) There cannot be any ties. Rank each person in his or her proper order.
2) No one should know where they are ranked. This information is yours alone.
3) No talking during the exercise.
4) If you write any sensitive information on paper, make sure no one sees it.

FACILITATOR NOTES:
This is not an easy activity and should be done with honesty and seriousness. There have been several groups I have worked with that refused to do this activity once they heard the instructions. If this happens to you, don't force people to finish the activity, but discuss what makes this activity so difficult. The discussion will lead to a conversation rich with answers and questions about trust.

The overall goal of this activity is to lead into a discussion of what people truly value about others that will increase trustworthiness. If someone is working toward being more trustworthy, this activity should offer some clear insight.

In all honesty, we do this activity in an informal way every day. We naturally determine if we can trust someone or not based on our own perceptions. Turning it into a formal exercise can make it seem uncomfortable and awkward. It reminds me of the kid in school who thought it was funny to announce that we were all naked under our clothes. Yes, but we don't usually think about it in that way.

VARIATIONS:
• Prepare a set of pictures of 5 or 6 people that everyone in the group would recognize. Project the pictures on an overhead and ask the participants to rank order the people in terms of their perceived trustworthiness.

POTENTIAL DISCUSSION QUESTIONS:
• Without mentioning names, what was it that made your most trustworthy person rank so high?

• What characteristics do you value most?

• What are some characteristics that some people ranked high that you don't see as valuable?

• In what ways have you been evaluating yourself during this activity?

Photo Finish

PROPS:
• Ropes or tape to mark the start and finish line (optional)
• Camera (optional)

OBJECTIVE:
Everyone on a team crosses a finish line at exactly the same time then discusses what caused them to pick their line judges.

HISTORY:
This activity comes from Feeding The Zircon Gorilla originally (Sikes, 1995). The task is deceptively difficult to complete because it challenges a team's ability to coordinate its movements.

PREPARATION:
Find a location that has approximately 30 feet between

a starting line and a finish line. A sidewalk, straight rope line, or line in the carpet or floor works well. Give the instructions to the team and stand at the finish line as the team does the activity.

INSTRUCTIONS:
Please choose two of your most trustworthy people. They will have a special role as you do the activity.

Notice how this is an unsuccessful attempt.
Some hands crossed after others.

This activity is called photo finish. Everyone must start behind the starting line and go toward the finish line, crossing the finish line at exactly the same time. Imagine the finish line is an invisible plane, as in American football, so that if anyone breaks the plane ahead or behind anyone else, you will have to return to the starting line and start again. The two people you selected as your most trustworthy members will be the line judges and they will be very tough when evaluating your performance. The team has an unlimited number of tries (although you might need to establish a time limit for the activity).

The Rules:
1) Start at the starting line.
2) Cross the line/plane at the finish at exactly the same time.
3) If everyone doesn't cross the finish at the same time, you must restart at the starting line.

FACILITATOR NOTES:
Most teams create a sense of urgency from the starting line to the finish. The truth is that time is not an important factor in this initiative.

Teams generally take about six or more "runs" before they finish simultaneously. I would encourage you to join in the line judge role. Some people that the team chooses may not fully understand their role to determine the all-way tie at first.

A camera or video camera is great to use and show the team later. One of the amazing things that I have noticed each time I have facilitated this activity is how far off the perceptions of the team can be. In some cases a person will finish two or three feet before the rest of the team and the whole team will believe they finished together.

Some teams get very frustrated as they work to overcome this challenge. I have had some teams use a line crossing aid such as pushing a table to help them cross at the same time. In most cases the teams succeed with small coordinated movements like a finger flick rather than big movements like stepping across. Often teams will challenge the rules and try things like one person crossing while everyone else is in contact with that person. I applaud the creativity, but reject the result. Everyone has to cross the finish line at the same time.

This activity seems too simple at first thought. Many organizations face similar situations all the time and realize too late that coordinating people can be a difficult achievement. For example, businesses try to provide training for everyone within a short time span, or a complex project needs to have everyone finish their deadlines in a coordinated fashion. In those situations, the same factors that create success in the photo finish will create success in real situations.

POTENTIAL DISCUSSION QUESTIONS:
• How did you finally succeed?

• What efforts did you make that really were not necessary?

• What was it about the two "most trustworthy" people caused you to choose them in the first place?

- Tell me about the interactions you had with your line judges?

- If you knew you were going to do this activity again, how would you choose your line judges?

- In what circumstances is it important to choose trustworthy people to hold people accountable?

"To dream anything that you want to dream. That's the beauty of the human mind. To do anything that you want to do. That is the strength of the human will. To trust yourself to test your limits. That is the courage to succeed."

    — Bernard Edmonds

Five Squares

PROPS:
• 5 envelopes with three particular pieces in each of them (See the templates for the squares below.)

OBJECTIVE:
As a team, construct five squares of equal size as quickly as you can from the shapes in the envelopes.

HISTORY:
This activity is credited to Dr. Alex Bavelas who used it in 1950 to study communication patterns in groups given a specific task. Although there have been several variations of his activity, it continues to give people insight into the benefits of giving, receiving, and trust.

PREPARATION:

Divide the 15 pieces into the five envelopes so that each envelope has three pieces. It is important that the three pieces cannot form a finished square. To make it easy, simply use the following number system from the pieces to stuff the envelopes:

Envelope 1 = pieces 9, 8, 5
Envelope 2 = pieces 1, 1, 1
Envelope 3 = pieces 1, 10, 3
Envelope 4= pieces 4, 6, 7
Envelope 5 = pieces 2, 6, 3

Divide the group into teams of five and arrange for each team to sit around a table so that they can see each other and hand pieces to each other.

INSTRUCTIONS:
"At your tables you will find five envelopes. In just a minute each of you will be able to open one envelope and see the pieces inside. Your task is to work at your table to piece together five squares of equal size. When complete, there will be a square in front of each player. Each of the squares will fit together without any holes or overlaps in the puzzle."

"During the construction time you may not talk or otherwise communicate with your other team members other than to give any one of them one of your pieces. You cannot take any pieces from anyone. No one can have more than four pieces at any time."

"This is a timed activity. We will be recording the finish time of each team so please raise your hands or get our attention when you finish."

The Rules:
1) No one can say anything or gesture in any way to communicate with fellow members.
2) No one can take or pull a piece from another member, unless he or she gives it to them.
3) You can give a piece to anyone you like by placing it in his hand.
4) You cannot refuse any piece you are given unless you

have four pieces already.

FACILITATOR NOTES:
Your presentation of this activity is important. Be sure to give all the rules and clarify questions before anyone opens an envelope. Once they get started, everyone is supposed to be quiet. The mood tends to be intense.

If you have too many people to divide evenly by five, feel free to assign extra people to be observers and report back during the discussion what they watched at their table.

This activity can be focused on a wide range of issues from problem solving to communication to trust. As far as trust, the dynamics that tend to come out usually follow a pattern of the players from: self (How can I make my square while giving away trash?), to others (How can I give my teammates what they need to be successful?). As a participant once said, "Give, so that another may give. Give with the trust that if you really need something, it'll come back to you for another will give it to you." People's competence for completing a square is often in question too.

Before the action starts, it is a good idea to show a quick demonstration of someone giving a piece to someone else (opened hand on table) and how to refuse a piece (closed hand on table).

The puzzle pieces can be copied to paper and cut out with scissors; however, I prefer using something more durable and reusable such as card stock, plastic, or matting board.

POTENTIAL DISCUSSION QUESTIONS:
• Did anyone break the rules?

• On a 1-10 scale, how much did you trust others in your team to help solve the puzzle?

• How did you feel about trusting others without talking?

• What was a critical turning point in this activity? What or who made it happen?

- Did anyone on your team obviously not trust the process? How could you tell?

- How does this activity illustrate how you do or do not trust others in general?

"Trust that life is giving you exactly what you need practice in."
— Anonymous

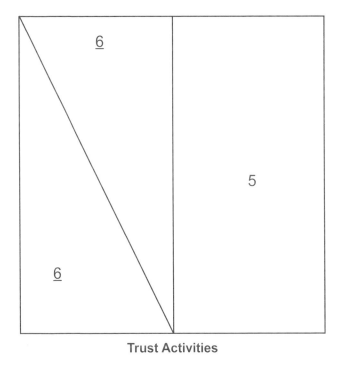

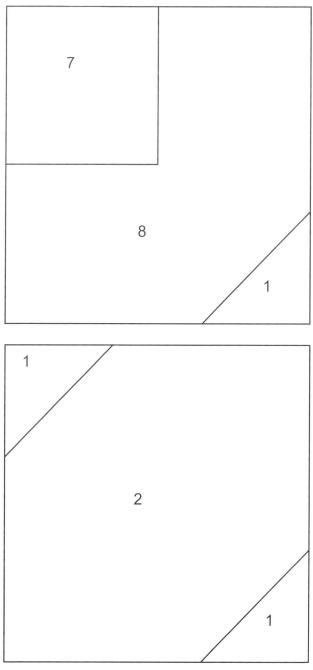

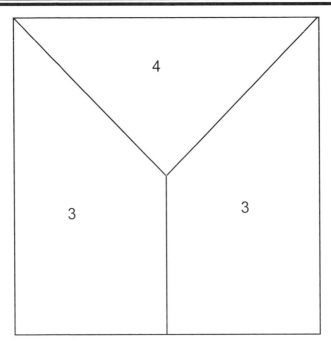

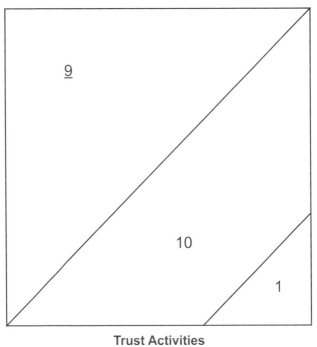

Mousetrap Trust Sequence

PROPS:
• 1 Mousetrap for each pair of people

OBJECTIVE:
Learn about trust, support, and coaching by setting and unsetting mousetraps.

HISTORY:
A few years ago I was asked to speak to a group and do some activities focused on trust and how we learn through experience. There would be more than 100 people and an hour to cover the material. Of course they also wanted it to be active even though the seats and tables were bolted to the floor. Looking at the training challenges, I knew the content needed to be something different. The result was the birth of this trust sequence

using mousetraps. The experience is like a Pamper Pole for your fingers.

PREPARATION:
Inspect your mousetraps for wear and tear and set them somewhere out of sight until you want people to get them. It is a good idea to have a few more traps than necessary in case any break.

INSTRUCTIONS:
Everyone find a partner and sit next to each other. Say "hello" to your partner then one of you needs to come get a mousetrap and return to your seat. We will be going through a 4-stage process using the mousetrap. (Explain to the group the true and false hazards of mousetraps on bodies. For example, a mousetrap will not remove fingers and they do not jump up to attach themselves to you. Also show and tell how to properly set a mousetrap.)

Stage 1: Set or Load the Trap (Approximately 3 minutes)
Partners should teach and coach each other to set the trap. Everyone should have an opportunity to set a trap.

Stage 2: Set or Load the Trap Blindly (Approximately 3 minutes)
Partners should teach and coach each other to set the trap while the "setter" has his eyes closed and the partner coaches verbally and visually.

Stage 3: Unset the Trap (Approximately 2 minutes)
One person holds his hand flat with fingers together and places his hand over the top of a loaded trap. Then, when he is ready, he lifts his hand quickly.

Stage 4: Unset the Trap Blindly (Approximately 4 minutes)

One person sets the trap, lays it on a table or floor, and coaches verbally while the partner unsets a trap as directed above, except that his eyes are closed the whole time.

FACILITATOR NOTES:

It is often a good idea to ask the group for a show of hands of who has ever set a mousetrap. It will give you an idea of what kind of pace to go through the steps. If a majority of the people has experience setting traps, you can spend less time on stages 1-3 and more on stage 4.

Often some pairs will finish a stage before everyone else. Feel free to challenge them to set a trap with one hand (no fair using a leg or table to stabilize the trap).

As a joke, I often say, "And for stage 5 you will need to unset the trap using your tongue...I call it 'outh' because that's what you say if the trap gets you."

POTENTIAL DISCUSSION QUESTIONS:
• How does this activity build trust?

• What changes have you noticed since you finished the stages?

• How did you overcome any anxieties?

• How well did you coach your partner?

"The people when rightly and fully trusted will return the trust."
— Abraham Lincoln

Faith Walk

PROPS:
• 2 or 3 mousetraps per participant

OBJECTIVE:
Three people take turns observing, guiding, and walking in an area of loaded mousetraps.

HISTORY:

The minefield activity has been used for many years to increase people's awareness and effectiveness in how they communicate and trust each other. This activity does not require anyone to be blind, but it does call for good communication, trust, and leadership. The idea of keeping people sighted changes the lessons between the walker and the guide. You also don't have to wash bandannas!

PREPARATION:

Ask everyone to take off their shoes and form a circle approximately 20 feet across with the shoes. Adjust depending on group size.

Ask everyone to set mousetraps and lay them loaded inside the circle in a random spacing relative to other traps. Some people may want others to set the traps, however, I have never had any trouble finding people who are happy to help.

Ask everyone to divide into groups of three.

INSTRUCTIONS:

There are three roles in this activity: an observer, a walker, and a guide. The observer should watch for subtle interactions between the walker and the guide with special attention to the walker's reactions to the behavior of the guide.

Only the walkers are allowed within the circle of shoes. The walker should focus only on his guide's eyes, without looking down at his own feet or the traps on the floor.

All the groups of three may begin simultaneously. The walkers should make their way across the circle, as best they can, while only looking into the eyes of the guide. The guide can give verbal and nonverbal commands from outside the circle.

When the walker completes the crossing, ask the trio to switch roles and continue.

FACILITATOR NOTES:
What often happens is that the walker will look down at the traps when the guide seems unsure or untrustworthy. Sometimes the walkers are unaware that they have glanced down. Some walkers and guides have more trouble than others.

The traps may seem like a real hazard. The only time they can be truly painful is if someone attempts to independently run through the traps. The wires, staples, and wood bases hurt like stepping on rocks. The snap is actually rare and being snapped is even less frequent. Even if someone is snapped, it just stings a little, but it doesn't injure.

VARIATIONS:
Ask for two sets of walkers and guides to do the activity while the remainder of the group observes. Give the

observers special instructions to look for what the guides and walkers do to create a trusting atmosphere during the crossing.

POTENTIAL DISCUSSION QUESTIONS:
• What did the observers gather about the guides and walkers?

• Which was the easiest of the three roles? Hardest? What made that true?

• What were the guides doing to instill confidence in the walkers?

• What were some strategies for getting across the circle?

• How did the traps affect your performance?

• What makes a good guide? Walker? Observer?

• How can trust affect your behavior?

"Men trust their ears less than their eyes."
— Herodotus

William Tell

PROPS:
- A rubber band (approximately 3 inches long and 1/8 inch wide)
- Plastic or foam cup or other unbreakable item to balance on each participant's head
- Glasses or safety glasses for each person

OBJECTIVE:
Knock an object off the head of a person by shooting a rubber band.

HISTORY:
Maybe it is because I am an only child, but I have no trouble entertaining myself. Growing up, I became quite skilled at killing flies with a rubber band. That skill has come in handy over the years whenever a rubber band war erupted at the office. (If you've never had a rubber band war, think indoor paintball in the offices or

conference room.) Yes, it's juvenile, but it is loads of fun and a great way to get rid of stress in a matter of minutes. The William Tell was created at a time when a co-worker and I were waiting for our office furniture in a new office space. Sometimes boredom is the mother of invention.

PREPARATION:
Find a hallway or nook wide enough for two people to sit across from each other comfortably leaning on the walls and still be close enough to shoot a cup with a rubber band.

INSTRUCTIONS:
Sit across from each other in the hallway. One of you will have a rubber band and the other will balance a cup on his head. Try to shoot the cup off your partner's head without hitting him. After he makes the shot, it's your turn. Play for a few minutes and consider how trust factors into this experience.

Feel free to practice a few times by shooting at a spot on the wall before shooting at the cup.

The Rules:
1) Wear your glasses.
2) Take turns trying to knock the cup off the top of each other's head.
3) Avoid blocking your face. If you have to, you may use your hands. As an extra challenge, try to keep your eyes open.

FACILITATOR NOTES:
This activity is scary, but it clearly illustrates the concepts of ability and willingness when it comes to trust. (See Situational Trust Model on page 11.) Can the person hit the cup off my head without hitting me? Are they going to hit me for the fun of it?

As long as people are wearing glasses, you need not worry about injury. It does sting a little if you are hit in the face, but getting hit is fairly rare. Most people, if they miss the cup, miss the person too. If a person wants to hold up his hands to block his face, that's fine. I only discourage using coats, books, etc., to block the rubber band because it removes the possibility of being hit and decreases the experience of the activity.

VARIATIONS:
• Turn the activity into a simple game by having each person shoot five times in turn with the winner hitting the cup off the most times.

• Let people change partners so that they can experience several people.

POTENTIAL DISCUSSION QUESTIONS:
• How did you help the other person succeed?

• When you were shooting, what was going through your mind?

• When you were being shot at, what was going through your mind?

• Who had only good intentions as you shot the rubber band?

• How did someone's ability to shoot accurately change your behavior?

• What happened when someone made a mistake?

"The people I distrust most are those who want to improve our lives but have only one course of action."

– Frank Herbert

Cutthroat Raptor

PROPS:
• 4-8 pool balls preferably in numeric order
• 1 snooker ball or cue ball
• 1 small flag or marker to identify the location of the hole

OBJECTIVE:
Get the snooker ball into the hole first by tossing your pool ball or eliminate your competition.

HISTORY:

The game of Raptor was designed to be played in a relatively small outdoor area and in a short time span, yet still offer a physical activity for up to eight people. (Sikes, 2003) Cutthroat Raptor is played as a competition so that everyone is against everyone and there are opportunities for temporary alliances among players. The name of the game comes from a scene in Jurassic Park where the velociraptors were hunting together in a tall grass field. As the people traveled through the grass, the raptors converged on them. The game mirrors that scene as the pool balls chase the snooker eventually to the hole.

PREPARATION:

Locate a relatively flat space approximately as small as a tennis court. The space can have some trees, rocks, and side walks, however, tall grass can make the game frustrating.

Take one of the pool balls and step on it to form an impression in the ground half the diameter of the ball. Sometimes a spoon helps to form a hole in hard ground.

Place a flag a few inches away to mark the hole's location.

Divide the balls so that everyone has their own unique ball.

INSTRUCTIONS:

This game has one small hole in the ground next to a marker flag, a different ball for each player, and a snooker ball. In order to win, one of you needs to knock the snooker ball into the hole so that it stays, or knock all of your opponent's billiard balls into the hole. There is no score, it is just a strategic win or lose situation.

To start a game, a player stands next to the hole and throws the snooker ball approximately thirty feet in any direction. Usually the person with the lowest number shoots first. The players take turns in numerical order throwing their own ball while standing next to the hole.

Whenever a person tosses his ball, if it doesn't hit another ball in the air or on the first bounce, it stays on the ground wherever it stops and the person's turn is finished. Other players may hit the ball when it is their turn, however, it should not be picked up again until it is that player's turn again or it is knocked into the hole.

Legal Shots

- Feet must be together and on the ground while shooting. No leaning on grass or other objects while shooting. You must release your ball before it contacts anything.
- After the first toss from beside the hole, all other shots should be made with the balls of your feet on the same location as your ball before you picked it up to make a shot.
- If you hit any other ball with yours in the air or on the first bounce you can shoot again.
- You may hit other balls for up to 3 clicks per turn (toss-click, toss-click, toss-click, done) If you miss on any shot or just roll into another ball, your turn is over until everyone has had their turn.
- The McAbee Maneuver is a special shooting technique perfected by Chuck McAbee. To get extra reach on a shot, a player may fall flat as long as his feet remain on the ground and the ball is  released before any other part of his body touches the ground. It can be painful.
- If one player's ball is knocked into the hole and another player's ball is butted up against it, the ball in the hole is out of the game and should be removed from the hole. If the second ball immediately falls into the hole too, it is

also removed from the game.
- If a player shoots his ball and it clicks on multiple balls on that one toss, it only counts as one click.

If a ball other than the snooker ball goes into the hole, it is taken completely out of play, even if it is your own, and that person's turn is skipped until the game is over.

If all but one of the opponents' balls goes into the hole, you <u>and</u> the other player win. If you hit the snooker ball into the hole, you alone win.

FACILITATOR NOTES:

For the purposes of discussing trust, I tell people that if the snooker ball is not knocked into the hole, but only two people remain in the game, the game is over and they share the victory. What this does is encourage participants to form alliances that may or may not be real. People can choose to risk and prove their trustworthiness...or not.

This activity is highly competitive. Once people start playing, the need for strategy becomes obvious. Unfortunately, the strategies can be about as simple as chess.

It is often a good idea to allow people to play more than one game if time allows. Even by the second game, people understand the game well enough to start effectively strategizing. Typically 30 minutes to an hour is enough time for people to get full value from the event.

An unusual dynamic often occurs in the activity. People will start trying to win by eliminating the competition even at the expense of knocking the snooker ball into the hole to win the game. The desire to beat someone somehow misdirects or redirects them into eliminating the other player's balls rather than simply putting the snooker in the hole. For example, a person may keep trying to knock in a certain competitor's ball (even though all are a threat when it becomes their turn) rather than just knocking in the snooker.

When presenting Raptor to a group for the first time, I wander around clarifying rules and encouraging good shots. If people want tips or best strategies, I tell them they have to ask just before they take a shot.

Some Raptor Terminology
<u>Snooker Ball</u> - A ball that no one tosses except to start the game. It is the one ball that will win the game when it is knocked into the hole. You can use a cue ball or an actual snooker ball with no numbers on it.

<u>Mule</u> - A person whose unofficial role is to hit the snooker ball back toward the hole. It is not a great role if the snooker ball is far away from the hole by itself.

<u>Castration</u> - When a person's ball is removed from play because it went into the hole.

VARIATIONS:
• Team play - The game can be played in teams. Simply have players play odd numbered balls versus even. Each person still plays with just one pool ball, but anyone on a team can win for the team by knocking in the snooker ball or eliminating the competition.

• If you have just two players, each player can use two pool balls so that it is similar to playing with four people. If you have three players, each can play with two balls so that it is like playing with six people. It is not a good idea to play with more than eight people or balls because the game takes too long.

• Play Indoors - Instead of a hole, just tape a piece of paper to the floor. When a ball stops on the paper, it is "in the hole." Tennis balls with twelve pennies inserted inside each can substitute for pool balls.

• I have played with different ball sizes. Golf balls require much more accuracy, bocce and crochet balls give you more range, and bowling balls are just plain scary. "Caveman Raptor," using bowling balls, is very fun and great exercise. I still prefer pool balls.

POTENTIAL DISCUSSION QUESTIONS:
• What changed from the start of the game to the finish?

• Did you prefer knocking the snooker ball in or eliminating the competition? Why?

• Describe some opportunities to trust in your game?

• How did you prove trustworthiness?

• When was trust broken?

• If we played another game, what would you do differently?

Hanging By A Thread

PROPS:
- Rope maker (See video at DoingWorks.com/movies.)
- 1 spool of cord for each team [I like to use 10 lb (4 kg test, 525 feet (160 meters) sisal cord]
- 1 spool of cord to use for demonstration
- Scissors
- Strong platform for the team to stand on and ropes or chains to connect the platform to the team's rope (The platform can be a variety of sturdy items. I have used

a pipe square with rounded edges, a 2x4 platform,
a tire swing, and a dolly frame. I travel, so I cannot
easily take a platform on the plane so I have had to
improvise.)
- Strong rope or chain to attach to a tree limb or beam
and the team's rope
- Pipe approximately 2 feet long and a torch or lighter
(optional)

OBJECTIVE:
Show teams how to make rope from twine then have
them make one by hand that can support the team. Not
only will they have to trust their new skills at rope making,
they will have to trust the rope to hold them.

HISTORY:
At a T.E.A.M. Conference in Chicago I went to a
workshop to learn to make rope. I was so amazed by

how simple it
really was that
I built a rope
maker in my
shop as soon
as I returned
home. The
machine to
make rope has
a variety of
pieces that can
be replaced
by hand
movements as
long as people
work as a team.

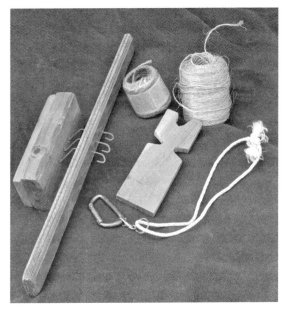

After many team successes at making a strong rope by hand, I just had to share this activity with a powerful trust message. It's amazing!

PREPARATION:
Locate a place to test the rope's strength when a team finishes making its rope. Look for a large tree with a strong branch sticking out far enough to avoid bumping into the tree or find a beam, pipe, or cable strong enough to handle the weight. It will need to be strong enough to hold an entire team at once. Get the site ready ahead of time so that you can answer questions during rope construction and everything will be ready to test when rope construction is complete.

Divide the group into teams of approximately six people. Since this activity will end by testing the rope with the team's weight, it will be important to divide the group so that their team weights at least look similar. The truth is that the same weight from team to team is not too much of a factor, but it will seem fair. Teams of six are ideal because everyone will have a role to play while building the rope.

INSTRUCTIONS:
(Watch this on video at DoingWorks.com/movies)
"Gather up so that everyone can see. I want to show you how to make a twisted three-strand rope like what you might buy at the store. It is a fairly simple process as long as you pay attention to the details. Do pay attention, because after I am done showing you how to make a rope, your team will be responsible for making one too."

"There are three main parts to a rope maker: a hand

crank, a hook swivel, and a cord separator. The hand crank turns and makes the three hooks turn in the same direction at the same speed. The hook swivel will hold all the cord and turn as the rope gets twisted enough from the crank. The cord separator keeps the cords of the rope separated so that they do not catch on each other and twist together before they should. It also regulates how firm the rope will be when it is finished."

"To make a rope, tie a small loop at the end of your cord. It is best to start at the end that is on the inside of your spool of cord. I am going to string this cord back and forth from the hand crank to the hook swivel at the length I want my rope. Neatness counts, so be sure all the cord pieces are even and at the same tension. Someone hold the hand crank still while I hook the loop on the left crank hook then string it to the hook swivel. Someone hold the hook swivel still and at the length from the hand crank you want your rope to be. Hook the cord on the hook swivel and string the cord back to the hand crank and hook it on the center hook. String the cord back to the hook swivel and hook it, then string it back to the hand crank and hook it on the right hook, then back to the hook swivel. At this point you will notice that there are two strands of cord on each of the hand crank hooks except the left one. I want a good-looking rope, so I want to put one more strand over to the left hook to even up the cord count. Once I string my cord back to the left hook, I could tie a loop and cut the cord to make a skinny rope or I could keep stringing the cord back and forth from left to right to make a thicker rope. If I had enough cord, I could keep going in the same way and make a really thick rope like the ones used on ships. However, for today I am going to do one more round so that I end up with four cords in each of my small lines. I will still end by going back to my left hand crank hook, tie a loop and cut the cord."

"Now I need someone to be a cord separator. You will hold onto the cord separator tool and make sure the three bundles of cords stay untangled. Slip the cord bundles into the three slots and the then slide the cord separator all the way to the hook swivel. You may want one other person to help keep the cord bundles separated by hand especially if the rope is longer. Before the person starts turning the hand crank you will need to determine which direction to turn the crank. Look carefully at the cords and decide which direction to turn so that it will tighten the individual cords rather than unraveling them. Once you are sure you know which direction to turn, start cranking. It will take quite a few turns before you notice anything happening. Make sure you keep a steady tension between the hand crank and the hook swivel and make sure the three bundles of cord don't grab each other. If they do, just stop cranking and the rope separators can pull them apart by hand. Continue cranking until you notice the cords at the hook swivel start to twist. Slide the cord separator away from the hook swivel a little and see if the three cord bundles start to twist into a rope. If they do, keep cranking, but start sliding the cord separator toward the hand crank. Make sure the hook swivel is able to turn. Sometimes you might have to help it turn. Notice that it turns in the same direction as the crank is turning. At this point, you have to watch the rope and try to make the three parts of the machine work together to make a beautiful rope. When the cord separator has slid all the way to the hand crank, stop cranking and get one of your people who were separating cord to whip the rope end so that it will not unravel when you cut it from the crank."

Wooden platform with rope supports

"To whip the rope, cut a piece of cord approximately two feet long and bend it over about three inches at the end. Hold the bent cord near the hand crank end of the rope with the bend pointing toward the crank. Start wrapping the long end of the two-foot cord around the rope and the bent cord about an inch from the end of the bend. Wrap it tightly, neatly, and toward the bend. When you are approximately a quarter inch from the bend, poke the end of the two-foot cord you have been wrapping through the bend and then pull the other end of the cord. The bend should tighten down and pull into the wraps you made. This should hold the end of the rope together. (See the whipping diagram on

Steel platform from old merry-go-round handle

page 111.) Trim the cord ends and then cut the three cord bundles attached to the hooks on the hand crank. The swivel hook can be removed now too, but you should not have to whip that end of the rope."

Burning the whiskers off the rope

"There are two more things you can do to the rope, but they are optional. One is burning the whiskers off the rope. The new rope will have many fibers sticking out of it. I use a lighter or a torch to singe off the whiskers. Don't worry about catching the whole rope on fire. The whiskers stop burning when they get to the rope from lack of oxygen. The last thing you can do is 'beam' the rope. Beaming simply means wrapping the rope around a pipe or round beam of wood and pulling the ends of the rope in a saw-like motion a few times. This helps the rope fibers settle into the rope and it helps distribute the tension throughout the rope."

Beaming a rope

The whole demonstration described above should take only five minutes. When you are finished with your demonstration

Rope ready to be tested

rope (which is only a half-inch thick and can be four or five feet long), ask for any questions and give the teams their assignment.

"Now that you have seen the process for making a rope, your challenge is to use a spool of cord and each other to make a rope 10 feet long and strong enough to hold your team's full weight when they are held off the ground by it. The only resources you have to make the rope are the cord, a pair of scissors, and whatever is on your person. That's right, your team will have to be the rope-making machine since you won't be able to use the one I used for the rope we just made. Feel free to look at the machine and ask questions."

The Challenge:
1) The finished rope needs to be approximately 10 feet (3 meters) long.
2) It will need to hold the entire weight of your team at

one time.

FACILITATOR NOTES:
Wander
around as
each team
works to make
its rope. If
you see that
they are going
down a path
that will take
a significant
amount of
extra time
or they don't
obviously
understand,
ask questions
that can get
them back
on the right
track. Most of the time the teams figure out how to make
the rope, but occasionally something significant doesn't
compute.

When the teams have finished their rope and whipped
the end, I usually have them beam and burn the whiskers
unless we run out of time. Teams will finish at different
times, so the beaming and burning naturally fill in the time
lag.

When everyone is done, gather the teams to the testing
area. I tie their rope into a loop using a fisherman's knot.

(See fisherman's knot diagram on page 112.) I then put the loop through the top anchor and clip into the two rope strands at the bottom. The bottom attachment is connected to the platform the team will be standing on. Ideally, the platform will be approximately 8-10 inches off the ground when everything is attached. For safety, ask that no one hold onto the newly made rope or anything above it. That way, if the rope should break, they will not get a rope burn. Also, make sure no one's body parts are below the platform at any time and make sure other observers stay close and spot the people hanging so that if someone loses his balance, he won't fall on the ground.

Most of the time the rope will hold the entire team. I have seen the rope hold ten adults. The few times it hasn't held, it was because the team tried to take shortcuts or simply did not work well together. If the rope does fail, the team will drop a few inches, but it is not a big impact.

After the activity and discussion, teams will often want to save their rope. Sometimes each person will take a piece of it home. They can whip the rope in several places and cut the rope between the whips so that each person can have their own intact piece.

If you want to use the rope for more activities, the rope can be used for any activity that needs a rope or boundary. If you need a strong circle to do a Raccoon Circle, just use a fisherman's knot to tie the rope.

POTENTIAL DISCUSSION QUESTIONS:
• How do you feel about what you just accomplished?

• What is it that made it possible to make the rope?

• Tell me how trust was demonstrated? (facilitator, new skills, team members, the rope itself)

• "A cord of three strands is not easily broken." What makes this quote true?

Making a quick hand crank, hook swivel, and cord separator

If you search the Internet, you can find a rope maker to purchase and you can even find plans to build your own. If you are not interested in making rope on a regular basis, or you just want something to make rope for this activity, below is a cheap and easy way to make it happen. Once you have made it, you can use it repeatedly. The tools you need are pliers to bend and cut wire, scissors, and tape. The building materials for the hand crank are a wire clothes hanger, two pieces of 4"x10" cardboard. For the cord separator you need two six-inch pieces of wood to make an X that you will need to glue, screw, or lash together or use the remaining part of your clothes hanger. The hook swivel can be anything the rope can latch into that will turn. My favorite is a dog leash swivel with a small keychain carabiner clipped onto the end.

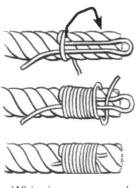

Whipping a rope end

(You can see the video of me making a rope maker at www.DoingWorks.com/movies)

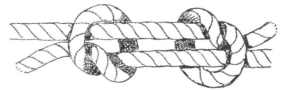

The fisherman's knot above is an easy way to
join the rope ends to make a circle.

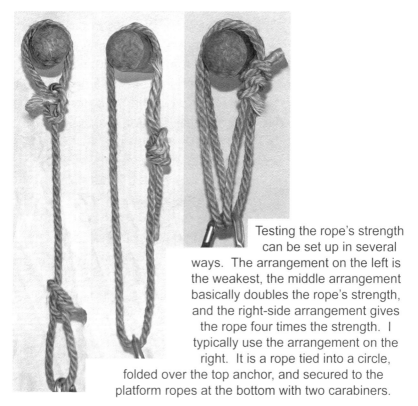

Testing the rope's strength
can be set up in several
ways. The arrangement on the left is
the weakest, the middle arrangement
basically doubles the rope's strength,
and the right-side arrangement gives
the rope four times the strength. I
typically use the arrangement on the
right. It is a rope tied into a circle,
folded over the top anchor, and secured to the
platform ropes at the bottom with two carabiners.

Introduction To The Last Three Activities

When training and teaching on the topic of trust it is easy for people to give head nods and lip service to what they will and won't do in relationships. There is a way to put people's behavior to the test with some activities that can (and usually do) show that, given the right situation, most people will make choices that help themselves and damage trust with others. It is a natural tendency, but one that can be intentionally overcome.

The following three activities are powerful tools to bring realism to a potentially theoretical topic. The activities are not meant to build trust. In fact, they usually cause people to be emotionally charged and sometimes behave in ways that surprise themselves and those that work with them.

The first activity I will describe is a classic. Many business schools use it as well as many trainers. I won't go into much detail with it because it has been written in many forms and there seem to be several "right" ways to facilitate it. The last two I developed and tested many times for the purposes of this book. Notice how all three create a structured environment for people to make choices for themselves or for the group as a whole.

Win As Much As You Can
Four teams choose to vote with a red card or green card. Depending on the combination of the four team color choices, money or points are won or lost.

You Betcha
Small teams make secret bids to win part of a large sum of money or points. If the sum of the bids is less than the total offered <u>and</u> teams' bids do not tie, each team gets their bid.

Community Chest
Teams start with a budget of money resources they may donate to a cause and they are assured that they will all receive an equal distribution, plus interest, of all the money donated.

"Anyone who goes through life trusting people without making sure they are worthy of trust is a fool. Yet there are people who may be trusted, men as well as women. There are as many differences in their natures as there are flowers in these meadows."

— Elizabeth Aston

Win As Much As You Can

PROPS:
4 green cards or markers
4 red cards or markers

OBJECTIVE:
To win as much as you can.

INSTRUCTIONS:
Divide into four teams with each team having a red card and a green card. There are 6-8 rounds to this game. For each round your team will choose to display either a red or green card. Cards are displayed simultaneously when called for by the game leader. The payoff for each round depends on the pattern of choices made by all four teams. The possible patterns and the payoff for each round are:

Scoring Per Round
4 red.......lose $100 each
3 red.......win $100 each 1 green...lose $100
2 red.......win $200 each 2 green...lose $200 each
1 red.......win $300 3 green...lose $100 each
4 green...win $100 each

The first 3-4 rounds are done with a short discussion among team members but not between teams.

The last 3-4 rounds are done with discussion between teams by team representatives (usually in a separate room or hallway) before the representatives rejoin their teams and the teams show their color decisions. Facilitators often create extra excitement by creating in any of the last few rounds, a double, triple, or even 10X score for that round such that the winnings and losses are multiplied for that round.

A common point to the activity is that the potential winnings for the "organization" are maximized if, on every round, they had all gone green versus going red.

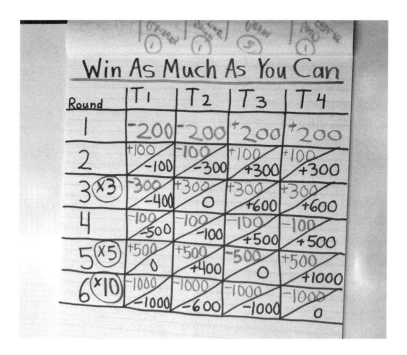

You Betcha

This activity brings out many issues and emotions that commonly occur in relationships. The activity itself is not designed to necessarily build trust, however, it is a great tool to bring to life real situations that can lead to trust, trustworthiness, and trust development discussions. At each decision point in the activity people are given an opportunity to choose whether to do what seems to help just themselves or help themselves and the group.

The simplest explanation of the activity can be illustrated with a candy bar, my two daughters, and me: I have a delicious candy bar that I am willing to share, but I want to creatively divide it. They are not allowed to communicate with each other. I tell them that they need to whisper a percentage of the candy they want, but they will need to think carefully because if their percentages are the same or add up to over 100%, I get to keep the entire candy bar. However, if their percentages are not the same and not over 100%, I will give them the portion they asked for and keep anything that remains for myself.

You Betcha is similar except you can have many more small teams (daughters) and they talk within their own small teams.

PROPS:
- Flip chart
- Markers
- Index cards
- Pens/pencils
- Calculator

PREPARATION:
Divide the group into small teams of 4-6 people.
Separate the teams with some space so that they can
talk quietly without being overheard. People will be in
these teams during the entire activity. Make sure each
team has a name or label so that you can manage the
activity more easily and so that the teams will develop a
sense of identity. Although you can facilitate this activity
alone, it helps to have another facilitator or a participant
who is not in one of the teams to assist you with the
math.

Make a chart to record the progress of the activity. The
simplest chart will have a header with **Money Up For
Bid**, **Bid Overall**, and **Facilitator Keeps**. Typically you
will be doing five rounds. The first two rounds will be
done by the teams independently, the next two rounds
with a representative from each team meeting together to
discuss, and the last round done independently.

Get a "significant" or "nice" prize for the winning team. A
prize, such as a bag of chocolates, works well because
the winning team has a final choice to keep their prize or
share their prize with the other teams.

INSTRUCTIONS:
Distribute five or six index cards to each small team and
ask them to put their team's name on each card. Explain
that they will be writing a bid amount on one of their
cards and turning it in to someone who will be collecting
cards from all the teams on each round of the activity.
Depending on the time you have scheduled for the
activity, you may have to set time limits on the teams to
write their bids.

RULES:

Every team will make a secret bid on an index card for each round. They will receive that bid as a score if no one else makes the same bid and the total of all the bids from all the teams is not higher than what is being offered. For example, if there were three teams bidding on $1000 and the secret bids were $333, $333, and $330, the total of the bids is $996 (less than $1000), but only the $330 bid would get to keep their money because the other two tied. As the facilitator, I would earn $670 since it is what remains of the money offered.

Write your bid on an index card labeled with your team's name. The bid must be kept secret from other teams and be in whole numbers.

Teams cannot communicate with other teams unless instructed by the facilitator.

The team with the highest score at the end of the game wins a nice prize and the satisfaction of being the winners.

FACILITATOR NOTES:
There is no magic to the amounts you choose for each round's bid. However, starting with a moderately high number on the first round then a small on the second round seems to work well. On the remaining rounds you may want to make sure it is possible for the outcome to favor any one of the team's chances to win by making what is up for bid large enough.

I never divulge any of the bids until the activity is completely over. I will keep my own list on a note card and circle the ones that get to keep their bid so that I can calculate each team's score at the end.

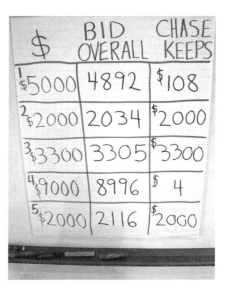

$	BID OVERALL	CHASE KEEPS
1 $5000	4892	$108
2 $2000	2034	$2000
3 $3300	3305	$3300
4 $9000	8996	$4
5 $2000	2116	$2000

When teams exceed the total of what is being offered in a round, the facilitator only keeps what was being offered, not the total of the bids. Also, when teams have duplicate bids, the facilitator only keeps what remains (what is up for bid minus what scores were won on that round) and informs the teams that bid duplicate amounts so they do not think they have more money than they actually have.

OBSERVATIONS:

Sometimes the focus will shift from teams competing against teams to teams competing against the facilitator. In other words, the teams will cooperate with each other to minimize what the facilitator keeps after a bid. Before the forth round I usually emphasize that the winner will be the team with the highest score, not the facilitator with the most money.

The dynamics that tend to occur in the activity include long, intense discussions within the teams before they place a bid, representatives agreeing on a shared plan then bidding higher on the actual bid, and using false totals when saying what a particular team's score is during representative discussions.

VARIATIONS:

Instead of money, use points. (It makes it easier for people to understand that there will be only one overall winner and they won't be splitting up the money at the end of game.)

POTENTIAL DISCUSSION QUESTIONS:

• How do you feel?

• What were some of the team strategies in this activity?

• What did allowing the representatives to meet do for the outcome?

• How did losing money to the facilitator affect your decision making?

Community Chest

PROPS:
• Index cards
• A pen or pencil for each team
• Flip chart paper to record the result of each round
• Calculator (optional if you do the math in your head)

OBJECTIVE:
The intended objective of the activity is for teams to "donate" money for a project that can benefit them all. Often the intended result is derailed by people's choices.

This activity comes from the world of economics. It can be done with as few as 5 individuals to over 15 small teams of 4 to 6 participants. What makes it a good activity for the subject of trust is the potential "opportunity" to achieve a very positive outcome, but also with the opportunity for people to be people and strain the relationships within the rules of the activity. Fairness, honesty, open communication, and win-lose competition tend to be some of the biggest challenges.

HISTORY:
I first presented this activity to a class of participants at the Black Hills Recreation Leadership Lab in South Dakota. Despite everyone knowing each other, the group dynamics were typical with accusations and self-centered decisions being made. The activity is an adaptation of the Public Goods game that is a standard of experimental economics.

PREPARATION:
Ask a couple of helpers to play the role of accountants.

They can be other facilitators or participants. The accountants will be gathering the secret bids, adding the totals, and figuring how much money each small team will be getting back after each round. You could do all this yourself without help, but it is difficult to manage.

On index cards, write a dollar amount that each organization will have available to invest (their initial budget). Don't make all the amounts the same and keep it confidential. I usually vary the amount from $500 all the

WATER PARK

Total Invested	Interest	Total Return	Return For Each
11875	25%	14843	2969
8038	200%	16076	3215
6042	0%	6042	1208
7540	300%	22620	4524
2015	500%	10075	2015

Notice how the total of all the donations are added together in each round, then increased by the percentage, then divided by the number of table teams.
$11875 x 1.25 = $14843
$14843 / 5 teams in this illustration = $2969

way up to $10,000. Depending on the number of teams, start several teams with a small dollar amount, a few in the medium range, and just one or two teams with a large amount like $10,000. If you only have three teams, make one small, one medium, and one large.

Create a blank flip chart similar to the filled-in one in the picture illustration. (See previous page.)

Divide the group into small teams of 4-6 people sitting in chairs or on the floor.

INSTRUCTIONS:
Multiple small teams will be asked to donate some of their money to a cause or project that they will share a benefit from. How much they donate is confidential. They will be asked for donations several times and offered a return on their "investment." The money donated plus the interest earned will be divided evenly by the number of teams and returned to all the teams.

The story you tell can be as imaginative and relevant to the participants as you like. The story needs to include what the small teams are (businesses, associations, investors, etc.) and an event or cause they will all benefit from. I often tell the story in the scenario below about a community water park that would attract new customers to town. It could be something like street lighting, wireless Internet, anything they can all benefit from regardless of whether they contribute or not. You will be asking for money that you assure them will be returned with interest.

The way the money will be redistributed should be written

for everyone to see and verbally explained without going into too many examples and explanations.

Here's the equation:
Your return = (Total of all investments + interest) divided by number of organizations

Return = (Total + Interest)/# of groups

Everyone gets an equal return.

No team can invest more than they have and they are under no obligation to invest any certain amount as long as it is whole numbers. (No change please.) A team's investment amount is always kept confidential. After each round, they can figure how much they have left to invest by simply taking what they got as a return minus what they invested and adding that to any money they didn't invest. (Some teams will earn money; some will lose money, but they don't know that.)

In the first two rounds, don't allow any team-to-team communication, but within the teams they can discuss freely. You might give a time limit for how long they have to write their investment amount on a blank card and turn it in, like 2 or 3 minutes, because the discussions tend to be lengthy otherwise.

On the next two or three rounds, allow a representative from each team to meet and discuss what they want to do in a separate location for 5 to 10 minutes, have them rejoin their teams, discuss for 2 or 3 minutes within the team, then write their investment amounts to turn in. The only difference in these rounds is that there is team-to-team communication through the representative.

If you have time, offer one last round without team-to-team communication and make the interest a huge amount (like 500%).

On each of the rounds, you as a facilitator can decide how much the interest will be. Don't reveal the percentage of interest until that round has started. I would suggest keeping it simple. My typical percentage for each round is 25%, 200%, 0%, and 300% then if you have time, one last round of 500% with no team to team communication on the last round. Assure the teams that the interest rate of return on each round is a 99.99% sure thing and their money is secure.

The Rules:
1) Your team may invest any portion of your budget (whole numbers please), but do not exceed what you have available.
2) Teams may not communicate with other teams unless instructed by the facilitator.
3) Keep track of the amount of money you have to invest. Subtract the money you donate and add the money that is returned to keep a running total.
4) All of your individual team's money amounts will be kept confidential
5) Write your donation amount on a card and turn it in when the time has expired for that round.

SCENARIO:
A nonprofit organization has recently been given ten acres of open land next to a river in the middle of a medium-sized town. At one time the land was an unused

wild area where some kids explored and played. In recent years however, the safety of the area has dropped and police arrests have become a weekly event. Our nonprofit has high hopes for reclaiming the land and helping to grow the town's economy by building a community water park.

We are asking for funds from this community of retailers. The way it works is we will offer to collect private investment dollars from each of your organizations to use in the various stages of construction of the water park. After each construction phase, we will be able to let you know how much of a return on your investment you can anticipate. We will take the total amount of the investment, plus any interest earned, and simply divide it evenly and give it back to you. So for instance, if there were only 3 businesses and each of them invested $100, that would be $300 total. If the interest was able to grow by 50%, the total would be $450. We would divide $450 by three and give each business $150.

(Total invested + interest)/# of businesses = Return

FACILITATOR NOTES:

Sometimes the connection to trust will be obvious. When team representatives meet on later rounds and end up not going with the agreed plan, teams can get upset. Even on early rounds, because each team has different starting amounts (and no one but you knows that), teams may start to think the situation is unfair. There is a tendency for teams to become selfish and forget that there may be a "greater good" they are funding.

Another issue that often becomes known is the "freeloader effect." A team may realize that if they contribute nothing, they will always come out ahead. This activity has a strong paradox; the less you contribute as a team, the more you gain monetarily, but if everyone contributes little or nothing, the investment (amusement park, wireless Internet, etc.) will fail to happen and everyone loses. The parallels to the concepts of redistribution of wealth and systems like government welfare programs are striking, and can make for lively discussion if it is brought up in conversation.

Another issue that often surfaces is the trust (or lack thereof) in the facilitator or money manager. A great discussion can be started on what you, as a facilitator, did to increase or decrease your trustworthiness during the exercise.

VARIATIONS:

• The amounts of interest for each round and the number of rounds are up to the facilitator and the time you have available. Large variations in the interest add to some of the excitement, but there is no "magic" to choose the amounts.

• Allow all the participants to listen to the representative discussion as if the representatives were in a fish bowl being observed. Only the representatives can communicate.

POTENTIAL DISCUSSION QUESTIONS:
• How do you feel?

• What were some of the team strategies in this activity?

• What did allowing the representatives to meet do for the outcome?

• Who won? (Remember, the objective was to donate to a common cause.)

• Excluding the crazy interest rates of return, what examples of this activity do you see in reality?

• What are the advantages to this donation system?

• What kept the donations from being higher?

"People who have given us their complete confidence believe that they have a right to ours. The inference is false, a gift confers no rights."

— Friedrich Nietzsche

Trustworthiness

Becoming Trustworthy

Developing your trustworthiness is a full-time job. The intent of this trustworthiness section is to give you and your participants a road map and headlights. The map is to help you stay on the path to being more trustworthy and the headlights are to illuminate where you may be in the dark. We all have those parts of us that we are unaware of or that we give little value to. Hopefully, working through this section will assist you and begin conversations to discover what you do well already and what you can improve.

Below are three categories that develop trustworthiness. They are your:
- **Knowledge, skills and abilities**
- **Personal Attitudes**
- **Certain Behavior**

From a facilitator perspective, the way to make the trustworthiness information valuable and "real" is to go through each part and discuss examples of each that the group generates. Afterwards, each person can rate himself, then work in small groups to develop an action plan for each person. The action planning in small groups works well because people often struggle to understand what they can do to improve by themselves.

Knowledge, Skills, and Abilities

Competence – the ability to do something successfully or efficiently

Be **competent** in what you are doing. Not that you are

being expected to know everything or do everything. But if you are a facilitator you should know how to manage group dynamics. If you are a plumber, you should know how to fix a leak. If you are learning or simply don't know, admit to what you don't know up front. Competence consistently comes up as the most important

factor in the study of trust. If you do not know how or what you are supposed to be doing, people have to rely on other people, besides you, and double check everything you are doing. If people are going to find you worthy of their trust, you are going to have to learn your job, position, or role. Avoid the temptation to try to fool people into thinking you have answers that you don't. It may be awkward at times to admit you don't know, but you are risking your trustworthiness otherwise. You may be able to trick some people for a while, but when your expertise is really needed, the truth will become obvious.

On a sliding scale of 1-5, where are you? 1=least competent 5=very competent

Personal Attitudes

Humility – a modest or low view of one's own importance; humbleness.

When you win, you say thank you and don't "bask in the glory." You don't play to the crowd or camera when you score the winning run or win the prize. You don't have to be first in line, or insist on being in charge regardless of your leadership abilities. You don't do something then say, "Don't you think I deserve a thank you for that?" or "Did you notice what I just did?" You graciously accept a complement. You accept victory modestly and lose with head held high. You are willing to ask questions and listen to the answers.

Jim Collins (2001), in his writing about Level 5 Leaders, says that the highest level of leaders in companies that go from good to great have a paradoxical combination of humility and will to get the job done.

Beware of the "humble brag." A humble brag is humbly seeking advice, while at the same time bragging about your situation. For example, I just dropped my kids off for a week at their grandparents. What will I do without them? My husband is really annoying me. He wants to be so involved in raising our child. How can I manage my money better when I keep getting promoted to higher paying positions? It might not be intentional, but the humble brag will not advance your mission of exercising humility in others' eyes.

On a sliding scale of 1-5, where are you? 1=least humble 5=very humble

<u>Gratefulness</u> – feeling or showing an appreciation of kindness; thankful

Don't whine about what you don't have or complain about what you do have. You value what you have been provided. You express appreciation to those who have sacrificed to help you. You view each day with a joyful attitude regardless of setbacks. You focus on the good things in your life and good qualities of people around you.

On a sliding scale of 1-5, where are you? 1=least grateful 5=very grateful

Behavior
<u>Generosity</u> – the quality of being kind and generous; giving time, talents, treasures

You realize that everything you have is not truly your own so it is easier to give away. You set aside a portion to give back. You offer the best portion or biggest piece or last cookie to someone else. You surrender your room or things to someone who needs them more. You look for things to make someone happy with what you have to offer. You "pay it forward." Open doors for others, give your seat to others, share. Your generosity can be a surprise and is not necessarily a true need of the receiver.

On a sliding scale of 1-5, where are you? 1=least generous 5=very generous

<u>Helpfulness</u> – giving or ready to give service or assistance

You must do chores or errands. Look for ways to help people up in life. You show you care. You know that your efforts will not always be recognized and you do them anyway. You help the host put things in order before leaving a gathering. You assume responsibility for yourself and offer help to others. Helpfulness is different from generosity in that it is fulfilling a need or task the person being helped is involved in.

On a sliding scale of 1-5, where are you? 1=least helpful 5=very helpful

Stewardship – to manage or look after

Take care of what you have so that it lasts. Take care of other's things you use or borrow. Eat healthily, clean your house, pay your bills, and don't go into debt. Organize your day, week, month, life, so that you can accomplish your responsibilities without overextending yourself. Think in terms of long-term benefits, not just what feels good now.

On a sliding scale of 1-5, where are you? 1=least care taking 5=very care taking

Transfer your responses to the scales below.				
Competence 1	2	3	4	5
Humility 1	2	3	4	5
Gratefulness 1	2	3	4	5
Generosity 1	2	3	4	5
Helpfulness 1	2	3	4	5
Stewardship 1	2	3	4	5

Look at your greatest strengths. What motivates you and keeps you doing these things?

Look at your lowest scores. What types of things could you do to make them better?

A recommended strategy is to name up to 3 very specific things you can do to become more trustworthy and work on those first.

**"It's funny, none of your references
can spell *trustworthy*."**

Helps: *Strategies for Staying Trustworthy*

Identifying those components we struggle with or excel in is just a first step in becoming more trustworthy. If I was able to keep all the commitments I made in a training session today, it would be great, but your trust in me will be diminished if tomorrow I am back to where I was before my training. In almost all developmental training, we set goals or action plan for ourselves. The struggle is following through with those plans. Because trustworthiness is such an important part of how we interact with literally everyone we encounter, I have included this section called Helps.

In economics, the Help is called a "commitment device." One issue is that the "present self" (the person in the training session, for example) creates a standard of behavior for the "future self" (the same person back at home, at work, or in society) as well as a consequence

for not living up to the standard. A challenge is that your future self is pretty smart and good at finding loopholes or simply justifying actions. Paying a fee for cussing in a meeting, scheduling feedback from others for losing weight, avoiding having snacks in the house, and cutting up all your credit cards so you stop charging are examples of commitment devices. These actions or arrangements are intended to help you stay committed by making it so undesirable to go back to the prior behavior, that you keep your promise.

To be trustworthy, many of us need certain Helps to begin new trustworthy behavior or maintain the behavior we already do. For example, I have struggled checking in online for a boarding pass on my favorite airline. I can get a boarding pass up to 24 hours ahead of my flight time and if I check in right at the 24 hour time, I get to board earlier and thus get more choices where I sit on the

plane. I am motivated to board earlier, but for some reason I often lose track of time and end up missing my early boarding opportunity. How can I keep this personal commitment? I use the alarm clock on my phone. It sounds simple enough, but I have discovered my Help had to be fine-tuned. Setting my alarm exactly 24 hours ahead of my fight time was not ideal because it took too much time to find my app, enter my name and confirmation number, and check-in (apparently there are many people that do this). So I started setting my alarm 5 minutes earlier. Unfortunately, I would too often turn off the alarm, get the check-in ready and politely finish any conversations I was having while waiting for the exact time, just to realize, much later, I had become distracted by the discussion and I would check in later than I wanted. I have discovered that one-minute before my check-in opportunity is just right. Since I started doing that, I have never missed my time.

You may say that you can keep the commitments you have made by shear willpower and don't need any of these external Helps. I would say, "Congratulations!" because you are one of a very few people in the world that can do that. Most of us need these external controls or constraints to help us follow-though on our commitments long term.

Russell Hardin (1996) divides the types of Helps into three categories: **Self-Trust**, **Social Constraints**, and **Institutional Constraints**.

The most familiar Helps will be in the <u>self-trust</u> category. They are strategies that help you keep yourself accountable. A few examples include:
- Post-it notes with a list of to-dos
- Inspirational messages to remind you of personal goals or how to behave
- An alarm clock to get you up on time in the morning
- A friend you take to a party that will remind you not to drink too much or stay too long
- A ridged routine to ensure you finish your chores
- A reminder message that pops up on your computer

Then we have <u>social constraints</u>. These are connected to values, beliefs and norms of the society you live in. When you use a social constraint, you risk disapproval from other people if you neglect your promises or commitments. A few examples are:
- Wearing a wedding ring if you are married.
- Joining a club or relationship and getting tattooed or even branded as a show of commitment to it
- Shaving your head as a sign of a life change.

- Moving to a part of the world or a different business that supports your goals.
- Wearing certain clothes such as a uniform or business suit.
- Shaking hands to "lock-in" an agreement or promise.

With social constraints, the point is to do something as a show of commitment that would be ridiculed if you broke the commitment. It would be as if someone wearing a fireman's uniform just stood back and watched as a  person lay on the floor unconscious. That a person is wearing the uniform compels them to take the actions expected by society, whether it is out of duty or to avoid the public outrage. Now, before you go out and shave your head and get a tattoo, realize that you can put yourself into a group or community with similar values, beliefs, and norms to what you aspire to because the rogue behavior will not be tolerated. You can join a community for your future self that will be supportive of your commitments and intolerant of things you want to avoid. The game plan is to fit your desired future actions into stable social constraints, especially social pressures of close relations.

Finally, there are the institutional constraints. These are typically binding agreements that involve a mutually

trusted third party. When you use an institutional constraint, you risk legal action, fines, or sanctions for not keeping your commitments. A few examples are:
- A rent agreement between a renter and a homeowner
- A lease agreement for a vehicle
- A bank loan
- An employment agreement

An institutional constraint makes you more trustworthy because, as an outsider or stranger, I know you will suffer fines, sanctions, lawsuits, or loss of freedoms from a third party if you do not follow through on what you agreed. In  effect, they reduce the risk of you being negligent of your obligations. It helps our relationship stay focused and less risky overall.

In all cases, the Helps create a situation in which we can be more worthy of someone's trust and more motivated to do the right things, be it showing up to work on time, staying faithful in marriage, or making the house payment.

The challenge and problem to solve is:
Which areas of trustworthiness are you needing to develop and what Helps will reasonably allow you to achieve them? The task will be unique to you, but feel

free to ask for assistance. Think of all the Helps you are already using. If some of them work particularly well for you, consider using similar ones on new situations you have committed to.

You will find a basic assessment of Trustworthiness at www.DoingWorks.com/trustworthy. It will be updated as people submit examples within each category.

Feel free to use it individually or with groups.

"Commitment means staying Loyal to what you said you were going to do long after the mood you said it in has left you."
                    - Unknown

This above all; to thine own self be true.
                    - William Shakespeare

Sample Trust Developing Schedules

The times below are approximate and the schedule will need breaks planned into it. Every group or team of people will have unique needs, This sample schedule simply shows a general sequence as an example.

Stand-alone Trust schedule:

10 Welcome and introductions

10 Icebreaker

5 Introduce topic of trust

15 Paper Folding activity

15 Introduce Situational Trust Model

30 William Tell activity and debrief using model

30 Situational Trust Model using examples and intensity

30 Where do you stand with others? (journal alone or discuss in pairs)

45 Create an action plan to develop trust with one or two other people. (small groups)

15 Close and thank-you

When including trust into a larger program, it helps to sequence it after people have had a chance to get to know each other and briefly build relationships (introductions and icebreakers) and experience how they handle tasks (problem-solving activities). In this way, the participants can put their trust experiences and discussions into the context of that team or group. A great time to challenge the participants to activities or situations that need higher levels of performance is after the trust portion. In this way, they can build upon and use everything they have been learning.

Within a program Trust schedule:

Welcome and introductions

Icebreakers

Problem-solving

Trust
30 Mousetrap Trust Sequence

30 Faith Walk

45 Leadership Trust Model introduction and discussion

More complex problem-solving

Action planning

Closure

About DoingWorks

At the core of every successful organization are individuals who understand and trust each other. Add common purpose and direction and you've created the team. Think of DoingWorks as an interpersonal tool to help your organization focus on its purpose and effectively realize its goals. Achieving this direction comes first by establishing a foundation where teamwork thrives.

DoingWorks focuses on the soft-skills critical for effective leaders, managers, team members, and the greater community. It was established in 2004 and is located near Austin, Texas.

DoingWorks makes it happen through experiential learning. Experience-based training and development methods are proven to engage the adult learner at a level that encourages long-term behavior change - the goal of all training programs.

DoingWorks, Inc.
351 CR 277
Liberty Hill, TX 78642

http://www.DoingWorks.com
512-230-0969

About The Author

Sam trains, facilitates, and speaks nationwide in a variety of corporate and educational settings including Fortune 500 companies, small businesses, and universities. Best known for his creativity, Sam has trained groups of as few as two people and as many as three thousand. He trains Ropes Course and business facilitators and develops related indoor and outdoor training activities for adults.

Sam holds a Master's Degree in Industrial/Organizational Psychology from the University of Tulsa, and a Bachelor's Degree in Psychology from Texas Tech University.

He is the President and Founder of DoingWorks, Inc. providing services and resources such as:

- Structured Training,
- Meeting Events/Conferences,
- Leadership Development,
- Team Building,
- Keynote Addresses,
- Train The Trainer programs
- Training Resources

Trainer Resources

These 38 activities have been effective with hundreds of work teams. Each experiential activity comes with facilitator and participant instructions. Includes game templates that may be copied.

204 pages - 6" X 9"

Feeding the Zircon Gorilla by Sam Sikes
ISBN: 978-0964654105

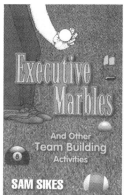

Contains complete instructions for a variety of activities to make your training meaningful and fun. The activities come with pictures, diagrams and a list of materials needed for each event. A matrix of learning objectives and another matrix of group sizes are provided for the activities.

224 pages - 5.5" X 8.5"

Executive Marbles by Sam Sikes
ISBN: 978-0964654129

Contains more than 40 new experiential activities including seven using mousetraps. Includes co-facilitation techniques that work as you facilitate and how to create your own activities. There are plenty of pictures and clear instructions.

224 pages - 6" X 9"

Raptor by Sam Sikes
ISBN: 978-0964654174

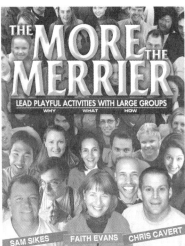

This book is as large as the groups it was written for. Weighing in at 2.6 pounds, there is a lot of information about facilitating large groups. Apart from the 100+ activities, it also includes theory with references and footnotes, practical planning and design tips, and stories from many trainers sharing their large group facilitation experiences.

432 pages - 8.5" X 11"

The More The Merrier by Sam Sikes, Faith Evans, and Chris Cavert ISBN: 978-0964654198

The "Noodle book" is a combination of adapted activities and newly created activities that use foam pool noodles as props. None of the activities is meant to do in the water. Approximately half of the book contains icebreaker and energizer games and the other half contains problem-solving activities.

216 pages - 5.5" X 8.5"

50 Ways To Use Your Noodle by Chris Cavert and Sam Sikes ISBN: 978-0964654112

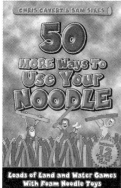

This new noodle book contains new games, problem-solving activities, water activities, variations and some "just for fun" activities. There are actually 55 more ways to use your noodle in the book, but who's counting? Also included are the plans for making your own noodle cutter!

208 pages - 5.5" X 8.5"

50 MORE Ways To Use Your Noodle by Chris Cavert and Sam Sikes ISBN: 978-0964654150

Other recommended books:

• *Engagement is Not Enough* by Keith Ayers

• *The Five Dysfunctions* of a Team by Patrick Lencioni

• *Good To Great* by Jim Collins

• *Processing Pinnacle* by Steve Simpson, Dan Miller, and Buzz Bocher

• *The Seven Habits of Highly Effective People* by Stephen R. Covey

• *The SPEED of Trust: The One Thing That Changes Everything* by Stephen M.R. Covey

• *A Teachable Moment* by Jim Cain, Michelle Cummings and Jennifer Stanchfield

• *The Thin Book of Trust* by Charles Feltman

Appendix

Blake & Mouton's Managerial Grid (1964)

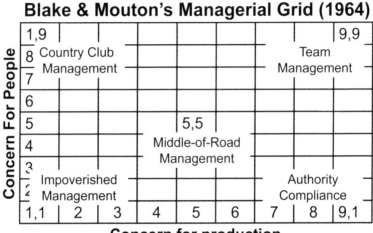

Situational Leadership (Hersey, Blanchard)

Supporting S3 For people with: High Competence Variable Commitment	**Coaching** S2 For people with: Some Competence Some Commitment
Delegating S4 For people with: High Competence High Commitment	**Directing** S1 For people with: Low Competence High Commitment

Little ---- **Supportive Behavior** ---- A Lot

Little ----- **Directive Behavior** ----- A Lot

Erik Erickson's Eight Stages of Human Development

Stage	Psychosocial Crisis	Basic Virtue	Age
1	Trust vs. mistrust	Hope	Infancy (0 to 1^1/$_2$)
2	Autonomy vs. shame	Will	Early Childhood (1^1/$_2$ to 3)
3	Initiative vs. guilt	Purpose	Play Age (3 to 5)
4	Industry vs. inferiority	Competency	School Age (5 to 12)
5	Ego Identity vs. Role Confusion	Fidelity	Adolescence (12 to 18)
6	Intimacy vs. isolation	Love	Young Adult (18 to 40)
7	Generativity vs. stagnation	Care	Adulthood (40 to 65)
8	Ego integrity vs. despair	Wisdom	Maturity (65+)

References

Ayers, K. (2006) *Engagement is Not Enough*, Advantage Media Group.

Blake, R., Mouton, J. (1964). *The Managerial Grid: The Key to Leadership Excellence*. Houston, TX: Gulf Publishing Co.

Blanchard, K. H., Zigarmi, P. and Zigarmi, D. (1985) *Leadership and the One Minute Manager: Increasing Effectiveness through Situational Leadership*. New York: Morrow.

Collins, J. C. (2001) *Good to Great: Why Some Companies Make the Leap--and Others Don't*. New York, NY: Harper Business

Covey, S. R. (1989) *The 7 Habits of Highly Effective People: Powerful Lessons in Personal Change.* Old Tappan, NJ, Free Pr.

Hardin, R. (1996) Trustworthiness, *Ethics*, 107(1), 26-42.

Hobbs, W. & Ewert, A. (2008). Having the right stuff: Investigating what makes a highly effective outdoor leader. In A. B. Young & J. Sibthorp (Eds.), Abstracts from the Coalition for Education in the Outdoors Ninth Biennial Research Symposium. Martinsville, IN: Coalition for Education in the Outdoors.

James, H. S. (August 2007). *World database of trust*. Retrieved from http//onemvweb.com

Kennedy, D. J. (1996) *Evangelism Explosion: equipping churches for friendship, evangelism, discipleship, and healthy growth.* Tyndale House Publishers

Livious (2012, October 28) *The oldest piggy banks are also the cutest.* Retrieved from http://www.thehistoryblog.com/archives/20945

Marston, W. M. (1928) *Emotions of Normal People.* New York: Kegan Paul Trench Trubner And Company, Ltd.

Mayer, R. C., Davis, J. H., & Schoorman, F. D. (1995). An integrative model of organizational trust. *Academy of Management Review*, 20, 709 –734.

Schuman, S. P. (1996). The role of facilitation in collaborative groups. p.33, In C. Huxham, ed., The Search for Collaborative Advantage. London: Sage.

Sikes, S. (1995) *Feeding the Zircon Gorilla and other teambuilding activities.* Tulsa, OK, Learning Unlimited.

Sikes, S. (2003) *Raptor and other teambuilding activities.* Tulsa, OK, Learning Unlimited.

Stromoski, R. (2014, August 7) *Soup To Nutz.* UniversalUclick

Amen.